DEVELOPING YOUR LEADERSHIP SKILLS

From *the* Changing World
To Changing *the* World

GUY MANSFIELD

CONTENTS

Way forward: While You Are Leading Changes.......149

References and Further Reading.................................159

FOREWORD

So much has been written about leadership that for many who are looking to develop as leaders, it is difficult to know where to start to learn! Accordingly, every chapter of this book is a distilled synthesis of other works on leadership which have then been summarised to give you an accelerated learning opportunity to develop as a leader. Leadership is mainly about making changes and that is what leaders do every day, everywhere, constantly changing parts of the world in a world that is continually changing. This book is to help you develop your leadership skills so that you can lead changes.

This book is principally for managers working in large organisations who have the potential and the drive to develop as leaders. The introduction enables you to consider your development potential and lets you assess how your organisation develops (or "selects") talent. You also need to reflect on how your organisation positions experts versus leaders and chose a development path accordingly. Your own development project should then be firmly anchored in the contextual reality of your organisation. Finally, in order to accelerate your development you need to slow down! This leadership development paradox is considered so that you can best learn how to develop your leadership skills.

This book takes you on a journey from *the* changing world to changing *the* world. In large organisations, focused on a particular business, there is a risk for managers that they become insular and introspective. Instead, they need to "reconnect" with the outside world-at-large, even more so now given the fast pace of change and the potential impact of those changes on any business at any level. The first section of the book therefore focuses on the changing world and the *need* for leadership; and in particular how *leadership* is different to *management* in relation to coping with change and uncertainty.

All leadership development projects should include self-reflection. Leadership is more about behaviours than skills so the next section of the journey looks at *you* and how to analyse your leadership behaviours today so as to possibly improve them for the future. Considering personality type preferences and interpersonal orientations and how they relate to leadership, this section also considers the importance of feedback and the expectations that followers have of their leaders. Different levels of leadership are considered before reflecting on the importance of emotional intelligence and different styles of leadership.

Leadership is however not just about you. As mentioned in the introduction, the organisational context is very important and so this next section of your development looks at organisational culture and what that can mean for leaders.

Invariably, leaders will have to adapt their leadership style not just to the particular follower but to a particular situation and this is considered here along with conflict resolution. Managers are often charged with large projects where they can only influence (rather than command) others to work. This section summarises how that can be achieved along with developing staff principally by coaching.

As business becomes more global, so too must leaders! Diversity is generally considered good for innovation and good for global business: but it is for leaders to include, leverage and benefit from that diversity. Considering the need for global leadership, the risks of "groupthink" and the benefits of diversity, this section of the book therefore focuses on how to lead across cultures and in particular how to lead diverse teams. Leaders will frequently have to engage temporary teams so in order to develop your leadership effectiveness this point is also reviewed along with leadership communication in modern global organisations.

By now you will be ready to learn how to lead changes! First considering creativity, this section then looks at innovation and in particular how to overcome common barriers to innovation. To effect change the leader needs to know about effective decision-making processes and decision biases. These are considered before turning how to "sell" your change project, how to lead changes and finally how to accelerate change. In reaching this stage you will have completed your leadership development journey from *the* changing world to changing *the* world.

Post-development, you have to deliver and then keep on delivering and so as an epilogue to your leadership development there are two more chapters: one on managing your energy to help you stay the course; and another on how to "stay on track" and avoid derailment.

INTRODUCTION:

LEADERSHIP DEVELOPMENT

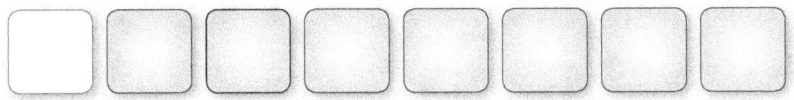

This section enables you to consider your development potential and lets you assess how your organisation develops (or "selects") talent. You also need to reflect on how your organisation positions experts versus leaders and chose a development path accordingly. Your own development project should then be firmly anchored in the contextual reality of your organisation. Finally, in order to accelerate your development you need to slow down! This leadership development paradox is considered so that you can best learn how to develop your leadership skills.

LEADERSHIP POTENTIAL

What is potential? In "How to Hang on to Your High Potentials" (October 2011, Harvard Business Review), the authors Fernandez-Araoz, Groysberg and Nohria suggest that potential is a person's "ability to grow and to handle responsibilities of greater scale and scope". Scale can be measured in terms of budget or staff; scope can be defined with reference to breadth and complexity. To identify this potential in a leadership context, the authors make reference to the Egon Zehnder International model for assessing potential for which the main parts are as follows:

LEADERSHIP POTENTIAL

Individual's Motives

This "inner core" predicts consistent patterns of behaviour over time, and relates to the "social motivators" – need for achievement, affiliation or influence. One key social motivator related to leadership is "socialised influence (or having a positive impact on others for the good of the larger organisation)."

Leadership Assets

"Assets" predict how far and how fast a leader can grow. The four key assets are "deriving insight", "engaging others", "demonstrating resolve" and "seeking understanding".

Sense of Identity

"Identity" is how the person sees themself on the "stage". Engaging with the future, those with high potential should envision a senior role to achieve one of the motivations (and not just for prestige or status).

Skills and Knowledge

Unlike the three "innermost" items which are hard to learn or change, skills and knowledge can be "easily" acquired. To assess potential, the *ability to learn and acquire new knowledge and skills* should be considered.

Some cultures are implicit, others are explicit. Reviewing potential with the individual concerned, communicating status and being transparent are all "success" factors of the above potential review and identification system. This process can work well in an explicit (sometimes known as "direct") culture whereas it is more of a challenge in an implicit (sometimes known as "indirect") culture. Similarly some cultures place more emphasis on the past rather than the present or the future. Accordingly it can become more of a challenge to review potential when the reference point is automatically past performance. In this context, there is also the perennial debate about "born" or "made". Implicit, past-orientated cultures might conjecture that leaders are "born" whereas explicit future-orientated cultures might postulate that leaders are "made". As the authors say, "select with care" and in a multicultural environment extra care has to be taken to communicate transparently and objectively across all cultures whether implicit, explicit, past, present or future orientated!

SELF–REFLECTION BEFORE YOU START TO DEVELOP AS A LEADER:

Where do you see yourself in the future? Carefully considering all the aspects of your own potential, how far do you see yourself advancing? Also consider the context and opportunities that you currently have and compare with your potential.

Before starting your leadership development, make sure you have considered your own project: where are you now and where do you want to go? Reflect on why you want to develop as well as how you want to develop.

LEADERSHIP DEVELOPMENT

Only 10% of the development of talent (leaders or oth-erwise) comes from training (or "education"): another 20% comes from "exposure" (such as special projects and ad-hoc assignments); whereas the 70% majority of develop-ment comes from experience which is otherwise known as "on the job" training (ref. below). Unfortunately however, it is rare when a large company can coordinate all three aspects to ensure an integrated and holistic development offer. Whilst there might be succession planning for key positions, plans rarely consider the experience as part of the development; more likely the next "experience" is con-sidered as a trial where the candidate will either "sink or swim". It is then left to the training department to take care of the "development".

Research into the possible root causes of this dilemma are reviewed in Morgan W. McCall Jr.'s book "High Flyers: Developing the Next Generation of Leaders", Harvard Business School Press, 1998. His extensive research of organisational cultures led him to conclude that there are two widespread, fundamental and self-perpetuating myths about leadership.

- The first is that "a single (and usually short) list of generic qualities can be used to describe all effective leaders and that those qualities are relatively stable over the course of a person's career." (In other words leaders are born rather than made.)

- The second is that those who have the "right stuff" will "through the survival of the fittest, eventually rise to the top." This becomes a self-perpetuating myth by those already at the "top".

As a solution to this problem, McCall highlights the need for a development culture and describes the difference between leadership *selection* and leadership *development*: the symptoms, the assumptions and implications.

LEADERSHIP DEVELOPMENT

Symptoms

Selection: once in challenging assignments, people are on their own. Performance reveals whether they really have the "right stuff".

Development: once in challenging assignments, people are given help to improve the chances that they will learn. The goal is to help people succeed.

Assumptions

Selection: Leadership attributes (or "competencies") are fixed. You either have them or you don't. Experience is used to test the attributes.

Development: Leadership attributes are complex and are acquired. What you don't have now, you might have later. Experience becomes the source of attributes.

Implications

Selection: Identify the key attributes and develop measures for them. Search for candidates with said attributes. Give them challenging assignments to test their skills. Darwinian: *survival* of the fittest.

Development: Identify the strategic challenges the leaders must face. Identify experiences which can prepare people for those challenges. Seek candidates who can learn from experience and support them to learn. "Agricultural": *development* of the fittest.

If any company wants to achieve strategic success, to attract, develop and retain talent, to innovate and successfully expatriate all nationalities, then there are some very strong arguments to move to a development culture to include experience as well as education and no longer rely on just leadership selection!

Everyone likes to believe that notwithstanding the quirks and foibles of their immediate boss, the boss of all bosses, (i.e. the person at the "top") must surely have the "right stuff"! In terms of corporate culture, it is not only the people at the "top" who perpetuate the myth, but people in the "system" who want to believe in the "system". This makes it particularly problematic to move from a leadership selection culture to a leadership development culture.

Many companies are looking to improve innovation; however when the leadership model is one of selection and therefore based on survival, in such an environment, most leaders will not take risks; they will not be creative; they will not step outside of their profession or "safety" zone; and they will not allocate any time to anything other than surviving. If leaders themselves are not allowed to fail in relative safety then creativity and innovation are bound to suffer. On the contrary, a development model could not only help the leaders to succeed and to learn, but for the whole organisation to learn and innovate!

SELF-REFLECTION BEFORE YOU START TO DEVELOP AS A LEADER:

If your organisation appears to have a selection culture and you'd prefer to see a development culture, then you don't necessarily have to change companies, but you might want to reflect on how you're going to change the culture in the long term! In the short term, the change can start with your team. Talent development is a key part of leadership. By developing others you can also develop yourself. Consider how you are going to take others along with you as you develop.

LEADERS AND EXPERTS

"Experts" are sometimes unwillingly forced to develop as managers and/or leaders, mostly because good performance is assumed to be an indicator of future leadership potential; whereas strong performance can simply be a reflection of technical expertise. Notwithstanding the development motives of the individual which may or may not be taken into account according to the corporate culture, there might be a case that the leader / expert dichotomy is influenced by national culture itself.

Laurent, in the "Cross cultural puzzle of international human resource management", in Human Resource Management, 1986, investigated the theory that in many cultures, to become a leader, you first have to be an expert. The hypothesis is that recruitment is based on technical skills and then development is based upon technical competence. First and foremost expertise, management is almost an afterthought! Laurent measured the positive response rate in various countries to a statement regarding the "expertise" of leaders. Here are the results:

LEADERS AND EXPERTS

The percentage of respondents who agreed with the statement that it is important for a leader to "have at hand precise answers to most of the questions that subordinates may raise about their work" can be categorised as follows;

Very Low (less than 40%) e.g. Great Britain 30%.
These national cultures have weak uncertainty avoidance and small power distance. In these cultures, experience can count as much as qualifications, uncertainty can be welcomed rather than controlled, and the education systems tend to point towards more generalist development.

Low (40 – 50 %) e.g. Germany 40%
These national cultures have strong uncertainty avoidance and small power distance. In these cultures, the professions are important and "management" would not be expected to give opinions beyond their "territory", but uncertainty can be avoided through processes.

High (50 – 60%) e.g. France 59%
These national cultures have strong uncertainty avoidance and large power distance. Beyond qualifications, the belief in expert knowledge is very

strong: the more expert the leader, the better able the organisation to cope with uncertainty in the future.

Very High (more than 60%) e.g. Indonesia 67%.
These national cultures have weak uncertainty avoidance and large power distance. Expertise and management go hand in hand so that the "strategic apex" of an organisation might be seen to be "wise", having an answer to any question presented by a subordinate.

Does this mean that except in Anglo-Saxon countries, leadership and management must essentially remain an extension of technical expertise? When these cultural norms are applied within their cultural "boundaries", then yes, it might seem futile to promote Anglo-Saxon leadership to (say) Indonesian companies in Indonesia staffed by Indonesians with Indonesian stakeholders. But what if the country of business is different than the country of origin, if the staff is multinational and the business partners are from other cultures? It might not be the time (in this example) to stop developing experts as managers and bring in more generalist leaders; however once the business becomes "global" it might no longer be a competitive advantage to maintain the status quo. It is a case of balance and adaptability!

In large multinational companies, besides cultural adaptation, it might also be wise to take heed of the individual's wishes and motivations regarding the development as an expert or a manager; however for an organisation to accept to develop "generalists" as managers there has to be a cultural acceptance that managers do not necessarily have to be experts. Similarly, to develop experts without forcing them to become managers or leaders will also take a certain amount of "cultural courage". For most large global organisations, there needs to be two separate and distinct development paths. The organisation will need both experts and generalists managers; there will be individuals who want to be one or the other but not both, so why not develop the two separately?

SELF-REFLECTION BEFORE YOU START TO DEVELOP AS A LEADER:

Are you an expert, a leader or both? Would you prefer to develop as a generalist and be willing and able to lead experts or would you prefer to remain in your domain and continue building your expertise?

Not everyone has to be a leader and not everyone wants to be a leader. Being a leader means different things in different cultures and this should be carefully considered before you embark on your leadership development.

LEADERSHIP DEVELOPMENT PARADOXES

When organisations realise that the world is changing quicker than they are and accordingly they need to adapt as soon as possible, among other things, leadership development becomes very important. How can the organisation develop leaders as of "yesterday"? In ever fast-moving Asia this is question which is often proposed to the Human Capital Leadership Institute (HCLI) of Singapore. They performed research in order to try and answer this and their results were published in the *HQ Asia, Redefining Business Leadership* magazine, 2012: "Five leadership paradoxes: Accelerating leadership development in Asia."

LEADERSHIP DEVELOPMENT PARADOXES

From every perspective of trying to find ways to accelerate leadership development, HCLI found that there were in fact five key paradoxes:

To foster learning, emphasise doing
Leaders learn most from undertaking challenging experiences. This can be in the form of special

projects, but the emphasis is on doing rather than education. Experience takes time!

To accelerate development, slow down

Learning is not as powerful without time to reflect on what has been learnt. Jumping from one assignment to the next without taking time to reflect will not accelerate leadership development.

To excel at the task, harness relationships

The main differentiator between top leaders and others is not intellectual ability but rather interpersonal ability. Relationships cannot be built overnight – long-term is the focus!

To achieve success, learn to fail

The key is to "fail young, fail cheap and never fail to learn." At the team or organisational level, putting in place a culture of both tolerance of and learning from failure can take time!

To develop greatness, practice humility

Leadership development is not just a journey from "a" to "b". The end point is constantly moving and evolves with time: great leaders have the humility to recognise that the journey is continual.

Whilst the research was performed in Asia, the above paradoxes could apply anywhere! There is no shortcut to developing leadership and "best practice" organisations accordingly target their leadership development in the medium to longer-term. The advice is also clear for the leaders of "tomorrow" who want to get "started" as soon as possible: it would be wise to take note of the points above and slow down, reflect, learn from failure, consolidate experience and relationships and above all be humble!

SELF-REFLECTION BEFORE YOU START TO DEVELOP AS A LEADER:

Before you start advance with your project and develop as a leader, ask yourself if you have incorporated a plan to learn from doing as well as from education? Have you built in time to reflect on your learnings as you progress? Do you have the opportunity to fail? Consider which relationships (if not all) need to be nurtured in respect of your long-term development. Finally, keep a sense of humility from now and henceforth!

1. LEADERSHIP AND:
THE CHANGING WORLD

This section of the book focuses on the changing world and the *need* for leadership; and in particular how *leadership* is different to *management* in relation to coping with change and uncertainty. The first chapters review how companies can survive in the long-term and in particular how important corporate culture is to ensure future growth. Change is the key to survival and the key to growth; and it is leaders who make change happen.

THE LIVING COMPANY

The world never stops changing and in the increasingly fast-paced dynamic the only constant is change itself! Despite the changing world, stakeholders in large companies often overlook the fact that nothing is permanent. In fact, the half-life of Fortune 500 companies is only approximately twelve years: in other words, through bankruptcy, break-up, mergers or acquisitions, 250 of today's largest companies will have disappeared in twelve years' time. Nevertheless those companies "which had started to expand after they had survived infancy – during which the mortality rate is extremely high – continued to live on average for another 20 to 30 years." So says Arie de Geus, former Corporate Planning Coordinator of Shell and author of "The Living Company: Habits for Survival in a Turbulent Business Environment" (2004) Harvard Business School.

De Geus concluded that many companies die because their "managers focus exclusively on producing goods and services and forget that the organisation is a community of human beings that is in business – any business – to stay alive". His research set out to learn about long-term corporate survival by studying companies older than Shell: only 27 companies worldwide had "survived" for more than

100 years and his research centred on what these 27 had in common. He found four "shared personality traits that could explain their longevity."

THE LIVING COMPANY

The four traits that lead to long-term survival are:

Conservatism in financing
The companies did not risk their capital gratuitously. Money in-hand allowed them to "snap up options when their competitors could not".

Sensitivity to the world around them
All the 27 companies demonstrated that they had been able to adapt themselves to changes in the world around them. They were good at learning and adapting.

Awareness of their identity
No matter how diversified they were, their employees all felt like parts of a whole. A sense of community is essential for long-term survival.

Tolerence of new ideas
The companies tolerated activities in the margin, encouraging autonomous experimentation. They recognised that new businesses may be entirely unrelated to existing businesses.

There appears to be a paradox of having a strong identity and yet continually adapting; however identity does not come from business and behaviours; rather it comes from "clearly stated" values. The former can change (sometimes completely) while the latter remain constant. In this context, financing conservatism should not be equated to risk avoidance. To ensure the organisation continues to live whilst the world continues to change, leaders "must place commitment to people before assets, respect for innovation before devotion to policy, [and] the messiness of learning before orderly procedures..."

In a competitive environment, companies need to be more agile, quicker at adapting and faster at learning than their competitors. Constantly reviewing the outside world, the focus is to develop potential whether that is through new business, innovation or the development of talent (individual, team and company-wide). De Geus talks of "stewardship" where leaders pass on the corporation to the next generation in the same or better "health" than it was before. In order to do so and to nurture the sense of community, leaders need to both trust others and be trusted: a particular challenge in the very fast changing and often short-term focused world of today!

CORPORATE CULTURE AND PERFORMANCE

Many large organisations lament the lack of innovation; the lack of agility; and the over centralisation of decision-making. A further analysis of these "ailments" often leads to the conclusion that performance is not as good as what it could be; in other words the company is not achieving its potential. If a lack of innovation, speed and empowerment are considered to be symptoms of a corporate culture then it seems that there might be a link between corporate culture and performance.

The answer as to whether there is a link or not is to be found in a book by Kotter and Heskett of the same title (1992, The Free Press). They specifically set out to determine whether there is a relationship between corporate culture and economic performance. The term "corporate culture" was relatively new at the time, but their findings are still pertinent, relevant and applicable today. The authors studied the culture of 207 companies and analysed their respective financial performance over an 11 year period (revenue growth, net income growth, and increase in stock value). There are three key findings:

CORPORATE CULTURE AND PERFORMANCE

Strong Cultures

A "strong" corporate culture is where "almost all managers share a set of relatively consistent value and methods of doing business". In particular, a new employee is as likely to be corrected by her subordinates as by her bosses if she violates the organisation's norms.

At best there could be seen to be a very-loose correlation between short-term performance and strong cultures. On the other hand, strong cultures are considered by analysts to be diametrically opposed to long-term economic performance.

Strategically Aligned Cultures

Here the content of the culture is more important than the strength of the culture. The corporate culture is only "good" if it "fits" its context. The context can be the business strategy or the "objective conditions of the industry".

The concept of "fit" appears to be useful in explaining short- to medium-term performance; however both the "fit" and the related performance appear to be temporary and cannot explain long-term economic performance.

> ## Adaptive Cultures
>
> Here "managers throughout the hierarchy provide leadership to initiate change in strategies and tactics whenever necessary to satisfy the legitimate interests of not just shareholders or customers or employees but all three."
>
> There is a strong correlation between adaptive cultures and long-term economic performance. 12 companies with the most adaptive cultures (compared to the 20 with the least) had better revenue growth at 682% (cf. 166%); better net income growth at 756% (cf. 1%); and better increase in stock value at 901% (cf. 74%).

So why doesn't every organisation adopt an *adaptive* culture? The reason a lot of large companies do not get there is "(1) a strong culture can blind people (even smart, experienced and successful executives) to facts that don't match its assumptions; and (2) an entrenched culture can make implementing new and different strategies very difficult".

Take for example, an initially "strategically aligned" culture: the firm performs well and there is no incentive to change or to be prepared for change. Management can become not only complacent but arrogant. Inevitably, the environment changes (regulations, competition etc.) and because the strategies and tactics are not developed and successfully implemented, the culture no longer "fits".

Performance deteriorates but there is no perceived crisis and the organisation tends to become stuck in a "strong" but-no-longer-appropriate culture, in other words and "unadaptive" culture.

ADAPTIVE AND UNADAPTIVE CULTURES

According to Kotter and Heskett, the difference between adaptive and unadaptive cultures can be explained with reference to two key dimensions:

Core Values

Adaptive cultures have managers who care deeply about customers, shareholders and employees. They also strongly value people and processes that can create change, e.g. leadership up and down the management hierarchy.

Unadaptive cultures have managers who care mainly about themselves, their immediate work group or their product. They value orderly risk-reducing management processes more highly than leadership initiative.

Common Behaviour

Adaptive cultures exhibit managers who pay close attention to all stakeholders and initiate change even if that involves taking some risks.

Unadaptive cultures exhibit managers who behave somewhat insularly, politically and bureaucratically. They do not adjust or take advantage of changes in their environment.

For an organisation to adopt an adaptive culture requires a long-term perspective and strong *leadership*. For the long-term, a robust leadership development program needs to be in place to balance management with leadership so that if (and when) change is required, there are the resources in place to achieve it *throughout* the organisation. In addition, usually precipitated by a crisis, the leadership initiative to change the corporate culture has to come from the top. This is the medium-term "project": an organisation has to ensure that tomorrow's leaders are ready to change. In particular, the best-placed individuals to effect the change are those who can maintain an "outsider's objective outlook" but have built a robust credibility and internal power-base whilst moving up the hierarchy.

LEADERSHIP AND UNCERTAINTY

What occasions and circumstances require "leadership" rather than other solutions (such as management)? When is leadership more effective than any other solution and how does that relate to the business environment? Keith Grint, a leadership professor, captures this concept of when leadership is necessary. The start point is that management is dealing with the "déjà vu" (seen this before) whereas leadership is dealing with "jamais vu" (never seen this before). Elaborating on this, Grint built a theory (which appears in the British Association of Medical Managers "Clinical Leader", 2008,) of how leadership is all about dealing with uncertainty.

Grint defines two key axes for analysing a given situation: one reflects the increasing level of uncertainty about a solution to a problem; the other reflects the increasing requirement of "collaborative compliance" required to achieve a solution. Moving across these two axes simultaneously, one can see the three following situations:

LEADERSHIP AND UNCERTAINTY

Command
There is no uncertainty about the solution as the crisis requires an immediate answer. To achieve a solution, coercion, physical strength or authority is required. The form of the "solution" is therefore "commanding" – providing answers.

Management
There is little uncertainty about the solution to the problem as it is usually a "tame" problem i.e. whilst possibly complicated, it has been seen before and is resolved in a linear fashion. To achieve a solution, "calculative compliance" is required using a rational process. The form of the "solution" is therefore "managing" – organising processes.

Leadership
There is high uncertainty about the solution to the problem as it is usually a "wicked" problem i.e. inevitably complex, contextual and with no clear link between cause and effect it might never have been seen before. To achieve a solution, authority is passed from the individual to the collective because only collective engagement can hope to address the problem (cf. "normative compliance"). The form of the "solution" is therefore "leadership" – asking questions.

It might look like the problems faced by any given business are "tame", but if you look again and put the business in the context of the complex and fast-changing, never-before-seen environment then it could be argued that all the problems faced by businesses today are "wicked". With the relative position changing every day, we therefore need leaders to constantly adapt the business towards an uncertain future.

Grint suggests the "irony" of leadership is that it is often avoided where it might seem the most necessary! Unfortunately, this seems apparent in large industrial companies where there is a legacy of "engineering mite" always having provided a solution to very complicated issues. Unfortunately, given that perfectly tried-and-tested processes are in place to solve "tame" issues, when a "wicked" problem comes along, it is often treated as another "tame" problem.

Grint elaborates on the questions to be asked to "achieve" leadership: think of reflecting rather than reacting; think of constructive dissent rather than destructive consent; think of empathy and collective intelligence rather than egoism and individual genius... and then you have the framework of questions to build "leadership" in an uncertain environment.

LEADERSHIP AND MANAGEMENT

Managers and leaders are different: "Manager's goals arise out of necessities rather than desires; they excel at diffusing conflicts between individuals and departments, placating all sides while ensuring that an organisation's day-to-day business gets done. Leaders, on the other hand, adopt personal, active attitudes towards goals. They look for the potential opportunities and rewards that lie around the corner, inspiring subordinates and firing up the creative process with their own energy. Their relationships with employees and co-workers are intense."

So said Abraham Zaleznik in his seminal 1977 Harvard Business Review article, "Managers and Leaders: Are They Different?" Reprint April 1992. His central argument was that businesses need both managers and leaders to survive but with too much management and not enough leadership, "a business will stagnate and rapidly lose competitive power." He categorises three main attitudes where leadership can be differentiated from management: attitudes to goals, to work and to others.

LEADERSHIP IS AN "ATTITUDE"

Attitudes towards goals

Managers' goals will be impersonal and deeply embedded in their company's culture and history.

Leaders adopt a personal attitude towards goals. By altering moods, evoking images and expectations and in establishing specific desires, the leader influences the way people think about what is possible, desirable and necessary.

Attitudes towards work

Managers coordinate and balance opposing views. Whilst diplomatic, managers can limit choices.

Leaders adopt fresh approaches to long-standing problems and open issues to new options. New thinking and new choices are proposed. Entrepreneurial and risk seeking, leaders are likely to become intolerant of mundane work.

Attitudes towards others

Managers seek out activity with other people but maintain a low level of emotional involvement.

Leaders focus on what the events and decisions mean to participants. Empathetic, leaders take in emotional signals and attract strong feelings of identity. Relating on a one-to-one rather than one-to-many basis can increase individual motivations.

The idea here regarding the attitudes is that the manager / leader can adopt one attitude at a time and as appropriate. Sometimes it is fully appropriate to be a manager: to solve problems in an objective and impersonal manner; other times it is more appropriate to be a leader: to be personally implicated in the goals, and consider how new options affect others. Sometimes the organizational culture might exhibit "management" rather than "leadership" attitudes. Some managers might therefore feel inhibited in demonstrating leadership attitudes; however this is the advantage of being able to apply the relevant attitude as appropriate. During the day-to-day course of business, during reporting and managing "upwards", the leader can be a manager; when however there are projects to run, changes to be made and staff to be motivated the leader can be a leader!

LEADERSHIP AND CHANGE

Kotter's 1990 article "What Leaders Really Do" (reprint R0111F, Harvard Business Review) builds on Zaleznik's themes and whilst clarifying the differences, he also emphasises that management and leadership are complimentary. Kotter suggests that management is about coping with *complexity* whereas leadership is about coping with *change*. They both involve deciding what needs to be done; creating networks of people to accomplish the objective; and then ensuring that the work actually gets done. However, managers and leaders achieve these tasks in different manners:

LEADERSHIP AND CHANGE

Planning and budgeting versus setting direction

Managers try to predict long-term orderly results from a complex environment.

Leaders have a vision of where the business ought to be in the future and direct strategies to achieve that goal.

<u>Organising and staffing versus aligning people</u>
Managers get the right people in the relevant positions to ensure processes and plans are followed correctly and efficiently.

Leaders constantly communicate their vision and strategy to all stakeholders and empower employees with a clear sense of direction.

<u>Controlling activities and solving problems versus motivating and inspiring</u>
Managers follow up on the plan, the budget and the process and then correct as necessary.

Leaders energise people – they inspire people with their vision and know how to motivate people at a human level.

As here and elsewhere, Kotter highlights that a lot of organizations are "over-managed and under-led"; however his message is not that management should be replaced by leadership – instead he states that good organizations need both "superb" management and "superb" leadership. Complex organizations can be made both reliable and efficient by "management" but should also be taken into the future ahead of the competition by collective "leadership" through constant change. If however "leadership" and "management" are mistakenly considered the same, then every time an organization needs more leadership all that will happen is that it will only "work harder to manage"...

2. LEADERSHIP AND:
YOU

All leadership development projects should include self-reflection. Leadership is more about behaviours than skills so this section of the journey looks at *you* and how to analyse your leadership behaviours today so as to possibly improve them for the future. Considering personality type preferences and interpersonal orientations and how they relate to leadership, this section also considers the importance of feedback and the expectations that followers have of their leaders. Different levels of leadership are considered before reflecting on the importance of emotional intelligence and different styles of leadership.

EXTROVERTED AND INTROVERTED LEADERS

Research into leadership development highlights that there is one key factor that differentiates leaders from others, and that is self-awareness. Many a debutant leader will therefore find themselves on a leadership development course with the results of an "auto diagnostic" tool such as the Myers Briggs Type Indicator® or equivalent. Amongst other things, the participant will learn that he or she is an "introvert" or an "extrovert". This is very useful information to increase self-awareness, but beyond that what does it mean in terms of leadership *per se*?

Much has been written on this subject and there is quite often an accent on the development of introverted leaders to become more extroverted (e.g. public speaking, etc.); but there is an interesting study in a book by Cain, "Quiet: the power of introverts in a world that can't stop talking", 2012, Crown. Cain cites Wharton Professor, Adam Grant who launched studies to test his hypothesis that extroverted leaders enhance group performance when employees are passive, but that introverted leaders are more effective with proactive employees. Here are the results:

EXTROVERTED AND INTROVERTED LEADERS

Two principle studies were conducted: 1. With a major pizza chain where the leadership style of the store manager was compared with weekly profits; and 2. Where teams competed with a menial task, but with two actors "planted" in each team to behave proactively or passively.

Extrovert Leadership

For the pizza chain study, extroverts achieved 16% higher profits – but only when "the employees were passive types who tended to do their job without exercising initiative".

For the menial task experiment, when the actors were instructed to act passively (which influenced the team's behaviour), extravert leaders outperformed introvert-led teams by 22%

Introvert Leadership

For the pizza chain study, when introverted leaders worked with employees who proactively tried to improve work procedures, their stores outperformed those led by extroverts by 14% higher profits.

For the menial task experiment, when the actors were instructed to act proactively and suggest alternative processes to the leader, introvert leaders outperformed extrovert-led teams by 24%

In order to maximise results the key seems to be either matching or adapting leadership behaviour to that of the followers. In general, Grant concludes that introverted leaders might wish to continue what they are doing, i.e. encouraging employees to take initiative. In particular, in order to take advantage of opportunities in a fast-changing world, organisations will have to rely more on employees who are capable of taking initiative and who therefore might be better led by introverts rather than extraverts. For extraverts in general, Grant suggests that "they may wish to adopt a more reserved, quiet style": it is important for companies to groom listeners as well as talkers for leadership roles!

The setting for Cain's book and Grant's studies was America. The central "lament" of Cain's book is that the USA has been moving progressively from a culture of "character" (reserved and dignified) to one of "personality" (talkative and gregarious). The book therefore proposes rebalancing an essentially extravert society with the virtues of introverted behaviours. In Europe however, the challenge is slightly different: many countries and cultures are primarily introverted. Referencing McCrae's work (2005) in such introverted cultures, there is actually more chance that the rare extrovert takes the lead.

For leadership development this can pose a slightly different challenge: in cultures which are used to a rare extrovert taking the lead, best performance might be achieved with passive followers! McCrae has postulated that this might suit an "authoritarian" culture with power being concentrated amongst the few (extravert) leaders. This might work well for maintaining stable and conservative systems or organisations; however it might not work as well for promoting innovation, seizing opportunities and staying ahead of the competition in the ever-changing world! European organisations therefore might do well to promote the development of leaders from their large pool of introverts so that they, in turn, can encourage pro-activity and innovation to better help the organisation approach the future!

LEADERSHIP, PERSONALITY AND CHANGE

In "Introduction to Type and Change" by Barger and Kirby, 2004, CPP Inc., the authors reviewed *inter alia*, "common" profiles for leaders in terms of the Myers Briggs Personality Type Indicator (MBTI®). Although the results should be treated with care as there is room for further research regarding cause and effect analysis, within the MBTI® framework, 70-80% of leaders prefer "thinking" to "intuition" and 70% prefer "judging" to "perceiving". Without going further into the details, the conclusion is that the "average" leader is likely to prefer "organising their external world in a logical manner": they like to get the facts, decide, plan and then get things done!

In the Journal of Personality and Social Psychology, 2005, vol 89, no 3, "Personality Profiles of Cultures: Aggregate Personality Traits", McCrae, Terracciano *et al*, reviewed 51 cultures to see if there was a correlation between average personality types and the respective group culture (which was usually, but not always, a "national" culture). One of the principle findings was that Europeans and Americans generally scored higher on "extraversion" than Asians and Africans. Given that the average leader in a Western organisation is therefore likely to be extravert as well as preferring "logical decision making in the external world", it might be worth noting the advice Barger and Kirby give on how to "deal" with these personalities in terms of change.

LEADERSHIP, PERSONALITY AND CHANGE

The authors proposed that (regardless of whether "intuitive" or "sensing") the following should be considered when dealing with extroverted thinking type-preferences during a change process:

Strengths and Weaknesses
Strengths are that they organise resources and people and then work hard to achieve set goals. They appear calm, confident and self-assured and are generally fair and consistent. *Weaknesses* are that they might tend to exclude others from the decision making process and may decide too quickly, moving to action before others are ready.

Influencing their behaviour
Identify the problem and its negative impact on the efficient achievement of the organisation's goals; identify possible solutions and the consequences of each as logically as possible; and

ask for what is needed, with a logical explanation for how getting it will make the change more effective.

> **What they want**
> Information which must be presented in a logical cause-and-effect manner. To be included in the decision process; in developing the plans; and in evaluating the results.

The above only relates to the expected mean personality type of a "leader" in a Western organisation. For any one organisation however the distribution can vary enormously from one "extreme" where there are clusters of this type of personality preference amongst the leaders due to industry or educational "norms"; through to the other "extreme" where all the leaders' personality preferences are as diverse as possible. Moreover, it is arguable that adaptive change in an organisation is more likely to occur when there are diverse personality preferences (where not everyone says or agrees to the same thing). In terms of leadership and change, this highlights a key paradigm:

Cultures tend to be self-replicating. In other words, those with the power in any group or organisation tend to replace themselves with those who demonstrate similar values and behaviours. Personality preferences are a key influence on behaviour. According to the statistics, leaders with preferences for "thinking" and "judging" therefore appear to be replacing themselves with other leaders who have the same preferences (hence the need for further research on cause and effect...). To the detriment of the diversity of personality preferences which by virtue of being diverse could assist change, the "old-guard" does not change...

So if the organisation does not already have a culture that is adaptive to change, how can leaders introduce change in order to become adaptive? For an average Western organisation, the answer can be found in "influencing their behaviour" (above)! This does however highlight the fact that to get out of the "groove" and make the initial change there has to be willingness and a motive amongst the external thinking types to increase personality diversity and move to a culture that is adaptive to change. The starting point seems to lie in presenting the information in a logical cause-and-effect manner...

LEADERSHIP AND INCLUSION

Inclusion is one of the three interpersonal needs identified by Shutz in his FIRO-B® personality inventory. The "Fundamental Interpersonal Relations Orientation – Behaviour" psychometric analysis also references control and affection. The inclusion need focuses on attention, recognition, association, belonging and acceptance. What is perhaps interesting in respect of leadership is the collective interpersonal needs of an organisation.

In Schnell and Hammers' "Introduction to the FIRO-B® instrument in organisations", 1997, OPP, their research findings indicate that in particular, the interpersonal needs of the leaders "will affect the climate or culture of the organisation. The organisational culture will reflect how each of the interpersonal needs is manifested in the organisation". For many large organisations, low inclusion, high control and low affection are particularly prevalent. Here's how such collective interpersonal needs affect organisational:

LEADERSHIP AND INCLUSION

In an organisation where the collective interpersonal needs of the leaders are "low" inclusion, "high" control and "low" affectation, in the culture there might be:

In respect of low inclusion:

- Barriers to the inner circle
- Resistance to diversity
- Formality that may interfere with creativity
- Limited consideration of others' ideas and opinions

In respect of high control:

- Blind obedience
- Concentration of power
- Overdependence of staff on managers
- Win/lose competition between individuals and departments

In respect of low affection:

- Doing only what is expected
- General level of pessimism
- Suppression of conflict
- Pervasive scepticism and testing of loyalties

How can such an organisation exist and what are the implications both generally and in terms of leadership? In terms of FIRO-B®, it is not just a need *per se* which is considered but the need in terms of "expressed" (i.e. how much the individual initiates the behaviour) and "wanted" (i.e. how much the individual wants the behaviour to be initiated by others). In a culture with a strong power distance (where there is a general acceptance that power is unequally distributed), there is a tendency for individuals to have both high expressed control and high wanted control. This is different to (say) an entrepreneurial environment where there would be a high expressed control, but low wanted control. Large formal organisations with strong hierarchies tend towards high control as the individuals within both express and want high control. As control becomes the main driver, both inclusion and affection might be neglected. Inclusion is often overlooked and affection can be relegated to third place in such a high control environment!

LEADERSHIP AND SELF-AWARENESS

Self-awareness is paramount for leadership development; however an increased self-knowledge of oneself is only part of the equation. What if your behaviours are seen by other people differently than how you understand them to be yourself? The matter is further complicated by the notion of conscious and unconscious awareness: there may be aspects of your behavior that might be critical for your success as a leader that you may not know about which others may (or may not) see! In relation to this, Joseph Luft and Harry Ingham devised what was later to become known as the "JoHari" window – a method for improving self-awareness. The model was first published in the "Proceedings of the Western Training Laboratory" by UCLA in 1955 and was further elaborated by Luft in later works. Here's a summary of the JoHari window:

LEADERSHIP AND SELF-AWARENESS

The model originally used 56 adjectives from which both the subject and their peers could select five or six to describe the person's behaviours. (Similar results can be obtained from performing a "360° feedback" exercise.) Results are then mapped onto a grid of four distinct areas:

Arena
What is known by the person about him/herself and is also known by others. Open, constructive and positive dialogue can both maintain and expand the open "arena".

Blind
What is not known by the person about him/herself but which is known by others. By seeking feedback from others, the aim should be to reduce this area and thereby increase the "arena".

Hidden
What is known by the person about him/herself but which is not known by others. Appropriate self-disclosure to reduce the hidden area can enable better trust, cooperation and understanding.

Unknown
What is not known by the person about him/herself and is also not known by others. Untapped potential can often remain here but can sometimes be found by trying new things.

There are many "auto-diagnostic" tools that a leader can use to increase his/her self-awareness however for anyone wishing to develop as a leader, it might be useful to consider embarking on a "360° feedback" exercise. The original JoHari model only considered peer feedback whereas 360° feedback will also consider direct reports and superiors: nevertheless, the essential spirit of the exercise is the same, namely to: 1/ reduce your "blind" spots by seeking feedback from others; and 2/ recognize what might appear hidden to others. The "unknowns" may still remain as such but what is important is the overall "improved" self-awareness. Knowing how you are seen (and not seen) by others is extremely useful for leaders as interpersonal relations are key to leadership.

As a leader and a manager you might have neither the time nor the resources for everyone in your team to perform a 360° feedback; however as a leader you will have a huge impact on what is in the collective "arena" of your team. For example, do people feel secure being "open" and "honest" about what they think and feel without fear of negative judgement? (Idem. for the "hidden" parts!) Is there a culture of both positive and negative feedback both giving and receiving? If not, how are the individuals going to collectively reduce their "blind" areas? Lastly, as a leader do you encourage and support others to try new things without the fear of failure? As a leader you have a direct impact on the culture of your organization and that in turn impacts the growth and development of others through self-awareness!

LEADERS AND FOLLOWERS

There is always a danger that leaders are developed "in a vacuum" without reference to what followers want or expect. A leader cannot lead without followers; but a strongly elitist system can often overlook the "role" of followers. This is addressed in an article by two INSEAD professors, Bartolomé and Laurent, "The Manager: Master and Servant of Power", Harvard Business Review, 1986. In their article they highlight the difference in perspectives between what "superiors" have of their "subordinate" and *vice versa*, including when a difference in perspective can be had by the same person.

LEADERS AND FOLLOWERS

The authors used comparable samples for both groups i.e. managers of similar ages being in similar hierarchical positions having both superiors and subordinates. One group was asked what they expected from their subordinates; the other what they expected from their superiors.

What managers expect from their subordinates
The percentage of managers who mentioned the following traits was as follows:

74% Good Task Performance

60% Loyalty and Obedience

53% Honesty

31% Initiative

In other words, the leaders expect their followers to principally perform well. Note however, that the "loyalty and obedience" can be at direct odds with the required "honesty" due to reticence on behalf of the subordinate.

What managers expect from their superiors

The percentage of managers who mentioned the following traits was as follows:

66% Good Communication and Feedback

60% Leadership

50% Encouragement and Support

37% Delegation and Autonomy

In other words the followers principally want to be led! Good communication, feedback, encouragement and support are all leadership "traits". The followers are not necessarily looking to be instructed or told what to do; but rather to be given direction and guidance.

The principal message of the article is empathy: the leaders can expect certain things from their followers but they also have to be aware of what the followers expect from them. Without this empathy, leadership itself can be rendered less effective due to expectation mismatches. In particular, the authors cite the issue of constructive feedback. This is wanted by the followers but seldom given; and for the leaders who expect "honesty", genuine feedback seldom flows "up" the hierarchy when there is not an effective leader-follower relationship. With the severing of this key information flow, new opportunities and possible innovations are often lost.

DIFFERENT LEVELS OF LEADERSHIP

Leadership development is relative: there does not appear to be a "standard" development that can be applied to any leader at any given moment. The leaders themselves and everyone else involved in the development process must know where the leaders are and where they need to go both from a personal and an organisational perspective. Different leaders are at different stages in their personal development and the organisation might have different leadership needs according to the applicable strategies and objectives at any one time. The different levels of leadership might be best explained by reference to John Maxwell's book entitled "The 5 Levels of Leadership: Proven Steps to Maximize Your Potential" (2011).

THE FIVE LEVELS OF LEADERSHIP

Position
People follow because they have to. The authority goes with the desk rather than the person.

Permission

People follow because they want to. This is the beginning of influence where people start to follow you voluntarily.

Production

People follow you because of what you have done for the organisation. It could be argued that this is performance in addition to the "permission" or influence.

People Development

People follow you because you have invested in them and developed them.

Pinnacle

People follow you because of what you are and what you represent. This mirrors the popular notion of "authenticity" in leadership theories.

Napoleon's definition of leadership was "first define reality then give hope". In large, complex corporations for leaders in a "position" level, there is a lot of emphasis on defining reality and not necessarily a lot of hope-giving! For the other levels, a common thread in Maxwell's book is the "giving of hope": with the emphasis on a potential future, people see that you are capable of achievement, that you can lead change, that you can develop talents and ultimately that you can have a vision and take people there.

Maxwell emphasises two very important points in terms of relative leadership development. When principally engaged as managers planning and organising complex tasks in complex environments, leaders can often overlook the levels "permission" and "people development". Position is literally just that and performance (or "production") can always be achieved with technical or expert skills in such an environment; but in order to genuinely progress as a leader, there has to be some ability to influence on a personal level howsoever that "influence" might manifest. In addition, for more "advanced" leaders, turning to their staff and becoming the leader of leaders-both-current-and-future is a good point of development to ensure that they and their organisation can reach their "pinnacle".

LEADERSHIP STYLES

There are many different leadership styles, but the question normally asked is when is each one most appropriate? The answer can be found in the most downloaded article in the Harvard Business Review library: Daniel Goleman's paper on "Leadership That Gets Results", March 2000. Drawing on his work on "Emotional Intelligence" (self-awareness, self-management, social awareness and social skill) and building on research by Hay/McBer, he identified six distinct leadership styles. The argument is that "leaders with the best results do not rely on only one leadership style."

LEADERSHIP STYLES

Coercive
This is the "do what I say" approach which can be very good in a crisis. It stems from a drive to achieve, initiate and self-control. The overall impact on the work climate is negative.

Authoritative
This is the "come with me" approach stating the overall vision/goal but leaving individuals to make their own

---

way. Stemming from self-confidence and empathy, the impact on work climate is very positive.

Affiliative

This is the "people come first" approach which builds team harmony and can improve morale. It stems from empathy and relationship building; the impact on work climate is positive.

Democratic

This is the "what do you think?" approach which builds consensus through participation. It stems from collaboration and communication and can have a positive impact on the work climate.

Pacesetting

This is the "do as I do, now" approach which works when leading highly self-motivated and very competent staff. Stemming from conscientiousness and drive to achieve, the overall impact on the work climate is otherwise negative.

Coaching

This is the "try this" approach focusing on personal development rather than immediate work tasks. It stems from empathy and self-awareness and has a positive impact on the work climate.

Goleman's theory is that these leadership styles are like golf clubs in the golf-pro's bag and as the leader plays the "game", the appropriate style should be selected for the appropriate moment. Given the effect of these leadership styles on the "work climate", and that fact that research showed a strong correlation between the use of more than one leadership style and superior financial performance, it is difficult to argue against this theory. What is particularly interesting is that Goleman asserts that the work climate starts with the leader: his or her leadership style will infuse the environment and have the consequential impact on the work climate. However, the leader might be somewhat restricted by the organizational culture as to what leadership styles can be used (in terms of appropriateness and effectiveness); then, the leadership style chosen will not only affect the work climate but reinforce the organizational culture.

For example, organizational cultures which have strong hierarchies are more likely to see "coercive" and "authoritative" leadership styles being used. The "coercive" style might be more prevalent in a formal (rather than informal) hierarchy where the authority goes with the desk rather than the person – no particular vision or goals are communicated: the leaders use the "do what I say" approach. This might suggest that the work climate in a formal hierarchy (using predominantly a "coercive" style) will be negative and as a consequence there might actually be a strong and urgent need for leaders to use other styles. The challenge to surmount this cultural barrier is however quite significant for example introducing "affiliative" or "democratic" approaches: empathy with staff and seeking consensus through participation might be anathema to that environment.

If the organizational culture does appear to limit the number of golf clubs in the golf-pro's bag, should leaders just "give up"? Should they only use the leadership style which is "easy" to effect in their particular environment? Certainly not! If any organization wants to survive in an ever-changing world, the organization itself needs to constantly adapt. Whilst the culture might make the choice more difficult, the leader can overcome this challenge. Work climate does begin with the leaders; so too financial results; and so too the culture itself. To return to the example of the formal hierarchy, in order to improve the work climate (and possibly improve financial performance) senior leaders should be encouraged to move more towards the "authoritative" style whilst generally, more junior leaders should be encouraged to use (for example) "democratic" and "coaching" styles in their own domains.

ORGANISATIONAL TYPE

Leadership does not happen in the abstract – it happens in context and for leaders in business, that context is usually the organisational culture. To be effective, the leader has to know the organisational culture with all its implications for getting things done. To understand organisational culture, a typology analysis was built by two researchers who addressed the concept of the organisation's internal and external focus. The Cameron and Quinn typology in "Diagnosing and Changing Organizational Culture: Based on the Competing Values Framework", 1999, was originally built by factor analysing large numbers of indicators of organisational performance. Finding certain "clusters" in their analysis, the indicators were further reduced to two dimensions, namely flexibility versus stability (in addition to the internal versus external focus). Here's the typology:

ORGANISATIONAL TYPE

Combining the key dimensions of flexibility/stability and internal/external focus, Cameron and Quinn identified four clear organisational "types":

Hierarchy

- These organisations are internally focused and stable.

- Accordingly they are structured and well-coordinated.

Clan

- These organisations are internally focused and flexible.

- Accordingly they are collaborative, friendly and family like.

Market

- These organisations are externally focused and stable.

- Accordingly they are competitive and results orientated.

Adhocracy

- These organisations are externally focused and flexible.

- Accordingly they are innovative, dynamic and entrepreneurial.

Reading the above, the implicit conclusion is that the "adhocracy" is best adapted to change; however, it is actually difficult to see which "type" is more applicable to a given environment at any one time since change is ubiquitous and a type "photograph" might not therefore represent the organisation "movie". But it is regarding change where this type analysis can be useful because a quick review can be conducted twice: once to capture the "as is" and secondly to capture the preferred "to be" type. Note however that the starting principle is that the poles of any dimension are in conflict with each other and must therefore be reconciled: accordingly, "to be" proposals might tend to gravitate towards the middle ground.

3. LEADERSHIP AND:
YOUR ORGANISATION

For leadership to be effective the organisational context is very important and so this section of your development looks at organisational culture and what that can mean for leaders. Invariably, leaders will have to adapt their leadership style not just to the particular follower but to a particular situation and this is considered here along with conflict resolution. Managers are often charged with large projects where they can only influence (rather than command) others to work. This section summarises how that can be achieved along with developing staff principally by coaching.

ORGANISATIONAL TYPE AND NATIONAL CULTURES

What about the link between organisational culture and national culture? In "Cultures and Organisations: Software of the Mind: Intercultural Cooperation and Its Importance for Survival", Hofstede et al, 2010, the authors take the organisational theories of Mintzberg and compare them with national cultures as determined by Hofstede's cultural dimensions. Mintzberg's research led him to identify five key "parts" of an organisation along with five preferred "coordinating mechanisms". Combining these into pairs led to the theory of five different organisational "configurations" (or "cultures"). Hofstede's research into the cultural dimensions of power distance (the acceptance of unequal power distribution) and uncertainty avoidance (the extent of discomfort with uncertainty) led to certain groupings of national cultures according to the nation's "position" on a graph when plotting the two dimensions against each other. Combining these two empirically extensive researches led to some interesting results:

ORGANISATIONAL CULTURES AND NATIONAL CULTURES

The five different organisational cultures show the following characteristics and relate to the following national cultural dimensions as follows:

Adhocracy

The key part is the support staff (people in staff roles supplying services) and the mechanism is "mutual adjustment" (of people through informal communication).

This corresponds with national cultures demonstrating low power distance and weak uncertainty avoidance. Example: Denmark.

Professional Bureaucracy

The key part is the operating core (the people who do the work) and the mechanism is the standardisation of skills (specifying the training required to perform the work).

This corresponds with national cultures demonstrating low power distance and strong uncertainty avoidance. Example: Austria.

Full Bureaucracy

The key part is the "technostructure" (the people supplying the ideas/expertise) and the mechanism is the standardisation of work processes (specifying the contents of work).

This corresponds with national cultures demonstrating high power distance and strong uncertainty avoidance. Example: France.

Simple Structure

The key part is the strategic apex (the top management) and the mechanism is the direct supervision (by a hierarchical superior).

This corresponds with national cultures demonstrating high power distance and low uncertainty avoidance. Example: China.

Divisionalised Form

The key part is the "middle line" (the hierarchy in between) and the mechanism is the standardisation of outputs (specifying the desired results).

This corresponds with national cultures demonstrating medium power distance and medium uncertainty avoidance. Example: USA.

Given the above, what is the best organisational culture for a multinational company? At first glance, it might appear to be the "divisionalised form" given that it is the only organisational "configuration" proposed by Mintzberg which is not situated at one of the "corners" (low-low,

low-high, high-low and high-high) of the plot as defined by Hofstede. However a closer look reveals that this organisational culture is not universal but rather suited to those national cultures that are neither low nor high on any of the national cultural dimensions: in other words, unique in their own way. This might be further evidenced by the popularity of management theories in the USA – according to Mintzberg this is where the power lies; however US management theories are not universally exportable worldwide – many "fail" in application because of cultural "friction". Leaders need to be very aware of this when operating globally, in a multicultural environment and/or in a multinational organisation.

SITUATIONAL LEADERSHIP

Besides adapting to the context and circumstance, leaders also have to adapt to the followers. One of the best ways of achieving this is with the help of Hersey and Blanchard's model of "Situational Leadership" (Hersey et al, "Management of Organisational Behaviour", 2007). This theory states that effective leadership is best achieved when the leaders adapt their *style* to the followers. Here is a summary of Situational Leadership:

SITUATIONAL LEADERSHIP

According to Hersey and Blanchard, different situations demand different leadership styles which are in turn, appropriate for a certain type of follower. The four styles are as follows:

Directing
High task focus, low relationship focus – the leaders define the roles and tasks for the follower, and supervise them closely. Decisions are made by the leader and announced, so communication is largely one-way. This is appropriate for low competence, high commitment

---

followers (making up in enthusiasm what they lack in skills).

Coaching

High task focus, high relationship focus – the leaders still define roles and tasks, but seek ideas and suggestions from the follower. Decisions remain the leader's prerogative, but communication is much more two-way. This is appropriate for followers who have some competence but lack commitment (needing supervision because they are still relatively inexperienced; but also needing support and praise to build involvement).

Supporting

Low task focus, high relationship focus – the leaders pass day-to-day decisions, such as task allocation and processes, to the follower. The leader facilitates and takes part in decisions, but control is with the follower. This is appropriate for followers who have high competence but variable commitment (not needing much direction because of their skills; but needing support to increase either their confidence or motivation).

Delegating

Low task focus, low relationship focus – the leaders are still involved in decisions and problem-solving, but control is with the follower. The follower decides when and how the leader will be involved. This is appropriate for followers who have high competence and high commitment (both able and willing to work on a project by themselves).

The key message is that effective leaders are versatile and can apply any leadership style at any given moment as appropriate; however not many leaders are capable of applying any style in any given situation. This might change however according to the leader and the organisational culture. The link might be that with situational leadership, there are two leadership styles which are low relationship focus: for organisational cultures which are high on individualism and masculinity and are essentially task rather than relationship driven, one might expect that there would be a tendency for "direction" and possibly "delegation" leadership styles rather than "support" or "coaching". When there is also a strong power-distance in the culture, leadership might be further restricted to "direction" rather than "delegation". In other words, in certain cases, the culture might restrict the ability of the leader to adapt to the follower. Leaders need to be aware of potential barriers to effective leadership and not just adapt to the situation but also to the culture.

CONFLICT RESOLUTION

Part of being a leader is dealing with conflicts. The "intuitive" response to conflict is "fight of flight" – either there is going to be a "win-lose" battle or one of the parties pre-concedes the battle by taking "flight". Thomas and Kilmann researched ways of dealing with conflict and concluded in their 1976 research that there were five approaches to conflict. This was further elaborated on by Thomas in the Journal of Organizational Behavior, (1992) "Conflict and conflict management: Reflections and update". The conflict management model now forms part of an "instrument" ("TKI®" by CPP) where the individual can assess conflict-handling behaviour according to this model. The five conflict-handling modes are as follows, followed by further implications.

CONFLICT RESOLUTION

In "conflict situations" (where "the concerns of two people appear to be incompatible") the person's behavior can be defined along two basic dimensions: assertiveness, the extent to which the individual attempts to satisfy his own concerns; and cooperativeness, the extent to which the individual attempts to satisfy the other person's concerns. These two basic dimensions of behavior thus define five specific conflict-handling modes.

Competing

Competing is assertive and uncooperative – an individual pursues his own concerns at the other person's expense. This is the "power-oriented" mode, being out to "win".

Accommodating

Accommodating is unassertive and cooperative – the opposite of competing. When accommodating, an individual neglects his own concerns to satisfy the concerns of the other person.

Avoiding

Avoiding is unassertive and uncooperative – the individual does not immediately pursue his own concerns or those of the other person. The conflict is not addressed.

Collaborating

Collaborating is both assertive and cooperative – the opposite of avoiding. Collaborating involves working with the other person to find a solution which fully satisfies the concerns of both persons.

> ## Compromising
> Compromising is intermediate in both assertiveness and cooperativeness. The objective is to find some expedient, mutually acceptable solution which partially satisfies both parties.

Many a junior manager may have been advised by a more "seasoned" colleague to not waste time "fighting the wrong battles"! Sometimes you just have to accommodate or avoid! As a solution, collaboration might sound ideal; however it's not always going to be applicable in every situation and might not always be worth the effort: sometimes compromises or accommodation might be the preferred modes of action. At the other end of the scale, one might be tempted to dismiss "competing" as too assertive without regard for other's perspective, but then when the "conflict" is corporate competition, there might not be enough space for more than one player in a particular market and the "win-lose battle" has to be fought. In all cases, it's a consideration of the context and environment that can influence the appropriate choice of conflict-handling behaviour.

Thomas and Kilmann built their model with reference to the earlier management model of Blake and Mouton wherein instead of assertiveness and cooperation there is concern for "production" and "people" as the two axes. Rather than conflict, Blake and Mouton referred to different management styles such as "production" (cf. competition), "impoverished" (cf. avoiding), "country club" (cf. accommodating), "middle of the road" (cf. compromising) and "team" (cf. collaborating). The latter might be particularly interesting for leaders – within an organization, leaders can be neither too assertive ("process orientated") nor too cooperative ("people orientated"): as usual, the ideal is getting the balance right, but not necessarily a compromise – the team comes together when concern for process and people are both high and there is collaboration!

LEADING WITH INFLUENCE

In an increasingly complex world the chances are that leaders will have to deal with stakeholders beyond their immediate "control". Projects often involve more than one organization working together according to the requirements of the business. Inside organizations, whether a particular task is successful or not will depend to a large extent on how leaders can engage people beyond their team. No longer being able to simply command or instruct others, leaders have to be able to influence. So how can leaders influence? An answer can be found in Cialdini's book "Influence: The Psychology of Persuasion" (2006) Collins Business Essentials. Here's how to influence:

LEADING WITH INFLUENCE

Cialdini is a social psychologist whose extensive research into behavior amongst "compliance professionals" led to the conclusion that there are six key "principles" of influencing:

Reciprocity

People are uncomfortable with feeling indebted. There is therefore a feeling of obligation to offer concessions to others if concessions have already been received.

Commitment

People have a strong desire to be consistent. For this reason, once committed to something, people are then more inclined to go through with it as it has become "congruent with self-image".

Social Proof

People assume that if other people are already doing something then it must be OK. Providing this so-called "social proof" can convince uncertain bystanders.

Liking

People are more likely to be influenced by those whom they like. Trust is a key factor of likeability, but people might like others simply because they have received compliments from them!

Authority

People will more likely accept the opinion of an expert. The authority referred to here can be likened to credibility – the more of which the person has, the more able they are to influence.

<u>Scarcity</u>
People are motivated by potential loss as well as potential gain. If something is limited in its availability and the "opportunity" might be lost, the perceived scarcity can increase demand.

Leaders require a lot of energy to convince and persuade people that a particular project or task is the one that people should follow! Any help a leader can get in order to influence should be welcome; however using these principles can come across as somewhat disingenuous if they are not used with discretion. Focusing on a short-term "win" at the expense of a long-term relationship might not be a good idea: reputations take a life-time to build and only a moment to lose! These influencing "principles" should therefore be used with care. Further, if people are persuaded to do things that are bad for them, it can be considered as "manipulation" rather than "influence" (with the former being unethical). As Drucker said, "leaders do the right thing" and in this context, the "principles" of influence can certainly help a leader in the increasingly complex world!

HOW TO LEAD BY COACHING

Peter Drucker once said that managers used to *tell* but in the future they will have to *ask*. If the corporate hierarchy is always telling the subordinates what to do (in an echo of school and military life) then how can anyone expect subordinates to take responsibility for their own actions, develop their competencies and realize their potential? The principle of coaching is to maximize the performance of the individual by unlocking their potential (which should not be confused with mentoring which is essentially experience transfer).

The process of coaching was itself first defined as "GROW" by John Whitmore. In his latest book, "Coaching for Performance: GROWing Human Potential and purpose – the principles and practices of coaching and leadership", 4th ed, 2012, his research shows that in order to retain the best staff, successful leaders lead in a coaching style rather than with "command and control". Similarly, management and leadership style determines the performance of staff: a coaching approach delivers the highest performance. Here's how to lead by coaching:

HOW TO LEAD BY COACHING

Within the context of increasing awareness and responsibility, there are four key steps to the process:

Goals

End goals should be distinguished from performance goals. An end-goal might be a dream or a motivator but can actually derail performance if set too high. Focus on the mid-to-long term performance goals.

Goals must be "owned" by the individual. They should be SMART (specific, measurable, achievable, realistic, timely), PURE (positive, understood, relevant, ethical) and CLEAR (challenging, legal, environmentally sound, appropriate, recorded).

Reality

In defining reality, be descriptive, not judgmental. Choice and control can only be exercised over what we are aware of, "but what we are unaware of controls us". The reality review is to try to move beyond symptoms to find causes.

Use "what, when, where, who and how much" to investigate rather than "why and how" (which can lead to conjecture, opinion and defensiveness). A thorough review of reality can sometimes throw up the "answers" before moving onto the next stages.

Options and Will

The purpose of options is not to have the "right" answer, but to create a list of as many alternative plans of action as possible. Avoid negative assumptions and hierarchising the options: instead objectively note the costs and benefits of each option at this stage.

The "will" is what the coachee will do: not "should" or "could", but will! Further, it needs to be defined when it will be done, who needs to know, what support is needed and how that support is going to be obtained. If anything is less than certain, consider adapting the "will" to make it certain.

Notice the fact that "goals" are reviewed and formulated before assessing "reality". It is quite often the case that reality is reviewed before setting goals, but as Whitmore says "goals based on current reality alone are liable to be negative, a response to a problem, limited by past performance, lacking in creativity or even counterproductive". Even if the leader is in an organization with a strong hierarchy, there is no reason for them to not coach their subordinates. Perpetuating the "command and control" by passing on orders is not going to maximize performance! Indeed, one of the key challenges for senior leaders is to develop talent and coaching is certainly one of the best ways to do so!

LEADERSHIP IN A GLOBAL CONTEXT

One article and one survey result, both coming from McKinsey Quarterly, highlight the need for diversity and leadership particularly when operating globally. In the article "Is there a payoff from top team diversity" April 2012, Barta et al., conclude from their studies that between 2008 and 2010, companies with more diverse teams were also top financial performers. Studying return on equity (RoE) and the earnings (EBIT) of 180 companies from France, Germany, the UK and the USA and comparing them with the number of women and foreign nationals on senior teams, they found that companies in the top quartile of executive-board diversity had an average of 53% greater RoE and 14% higher EBIT than those of the least diverse companies.

In the survey of 4,666 executives at global companies, Acquila et al., conclude in "Managing at global scale" June 2012, that the respondents are "satisfied with their organisation's overall capabilities but see room to improve in innovation and motivation. Better leaders are key." Regardless of the company type or current performance, respondents indicated that "developing leaders who are culturally and functionally proficient across regions is a key to more effective multiregional operations." Whilst reviewing the survey results for local strengths, organic growth advantages, and operational scale, the survey also focused on how executives thought that operations could be improved. Here's a summary of ways to improve operations:

LEADERSHIP IN A GLOBAL CONTEXT

The top six suggestions by percentage of respondents who selected each statement as a way to make their organisation's operations more effective are:

1. Develop leaders who are culturally and functionally proficient across regions

2. Improve formal and informal networks to maximise use of expertise across divisions and/or regions

3. Drive innovation more effectively across regions and divisions

4. Adapt organisational structure to improve balance between global standardisation and local responsiveness

5. Strengthen performance culture and performance-management practices

6. Build capabilities in a few key value creating processes and roll them out globally

Some of these are easier said than done (such as "driving" innovation); some are classic global/local dilemmas which are always a challenge (such as points number four and six); and some are more visionary than concrete (such as points two and five). However, they all come under the context of "global" leadership and the first point clearly summarizes it with a feasible objective. As the authors state, better "leaders" are key when operating globally. What the respondents appear to want is more culturally "proficient" leaders who can effectively work across different national and corporate cultures. This desired improvement appeared to apply to all companies including those who were already succeeding with a global strategy. For a global company, besides education, exposure and experience, cultural proficiency amongst leaders might be more easily achieved by having a diverse talent pool from which to identify, select and develop leaders. Leadership and diversity appear to go hand-in-hand in a global context.

4. LEADERSHIP AND:
GLOBAL BUSINESS

As business becomes more global, so too must leaders! Diversity is generally considered good for innovation and good for global business: but it is for leaders to include, leverage and benefit from that diversity. Considering the need for global leadership, the risks of "groupthink" and the benefits of diversity, this section focuses on how to lead across cultures and in particular how to lead diverse teams. Leaders will frequently have to engage temporary teams so in order to develop your leadership effectiveness this point is also reviewed along with leadership communication in modern global organisations.

GROUPTHINK AND THE NEED FOR LEADERSHIP

Groupthink is a psychological phenomenon that occurs when the desire for consensus in a decision making group overrides the members' motivation to realistically appraise alternatives. From the smallest group up to large organisations, groupthink can reduce creativity, inhibit innovation and result in sub-optimal performance, possibly even to the point of self-destruction (cf. Enron etc.) Why does this happen and how can it be avoided?

In an article by Powell, "Stop Groupthink Damaging Your Business", Finance and Management, ICAEW, November 2011, the author draws on the original work by Janis and cites three "antecedent" conditions to groupthink: 1/ High group cohesiveness; 2/ Structural faults (such as insulation, lack of impartial leadership and sociological and/or ideological homogeneity); and 3/ Situational context (such as highly stressful external threats, recent failures and difficult decision-making processes). Here are the symptoms and possible solutions:

GROUPTHINK AND THE NEED FOR LEADERSHIP

According to Janis, there are eight symptoms of groupthink:

1. Illusions of invulnerability creating excessive optimism.

2. Unquestioning belief in the morality of the group.

3. Rationalising warnings that might challenge the group's assumptions.

4. Stereotyping those who are opposed to the group as weak, spiteful, ignorant...

5. Self-censorship of ideas that deviate from the group consensus.

6. Illusions of unanimity where silence is viewed as agreement.

7. Direct pressure to conform placed on any "disloyal" members of the group.

8. Self-appointed members, "mind guards", shield the group from dissenting information.

Taking these into account and reviewing current research, Powell suggests various solutions:

1. Encourage diversity

2. Avoid directive leadership

3. Embrace the culture of enquiry

4. Don't chase consensus; rather explore disagreements

5. Do not isolate yourself from the ideas of others

6. Discuss issues in the spirit of openness

7. Avoid converging on an answer too quickly

8. Learn to deal with ambiguity

When seeing that sociological and/or ideological homogeneity is an antecedent for groupthink, it seems almost obvious that diversity is a solution; however is an "injection" of diversity an immediate remedy? On a small group basis: probably yes – diversify the members and groupthink might evaporate. On a large organisation basis: perhaps not – diversity might be prevalent in the organisation but it still might not be immediately included in the decision making groups.

When the decision of who can join the decision making group is subject to groupthink itself then the organisation is probably never going to benefit from increased diversity; instead the group will self-replicate and groupthink will continue. This is evidenced in many organisations where the diversity at entry level is very high but then steadily diminishes in direct inverse relation to seniority in the organisation.

Diversity is not just about nationality and gender: it is also about beliefs, values and behaviours. An organisation can therefore have lots of visible sociological diversity but very little ideological diversity. The organisation believes it is diverse but is only recruiting into its upper ranks new members who share the same ideology as the former members despite their nationality or gender.

A key form of diversity is to be found in different leadership styles. If there is only one leadership style and that is principally directive then dissent, discussion and open review are unlikely to be encouraged; instead the risks of groupthink and diversity exclusion are both increased. Diversity is needed to remedy groupthink; but for it to have an effect in large organisations, diverse leadership is also needed.

LEADING ACROSS CULTURES

In order to lead across cultures it is not only "local" cultural knowledge which is required but "global" cultural intelligence. In an article from Rockstuhl et al, "Leader-Member Exchange (LMX) and Culture: a Meta-Analysis of Correlates of LMX across 23 Countries", 2012, American Psychological Association, the authors reviewed the quality of leadership (low, medium or high) as per various LMX studies according to the national cultural values of where the study had been conducted. The results were further synthesized according to "horizontal-individualistic" cultures (low power-distance acceptance and individualistic, e.g. "Western") and "vertical-collectivist" cultures (high power-distance acceptance and collectivist, e.g. "Asian"). Here's a summary of leadership quality assessment which was NOT different according to culture:

LEADING ACROSS CULTURES

The research showed that the relationship between LMX and the following three items were NOT different in Western and Asian cultures:

Task Performance

The results showed that members of both cultural configurations appear to require the necessary work-related information and resources afforded by higher quality leadership to perform well.

Commitment

It appears that followers from both cultures perceive their leaders to be acting as agents of their organizations, thus commitment appears to be inspired by the quality of the leadership.

Transformational Leadership

The conjecture is that because of their "appeal", transformational rather than "transactional" leaders are more effective across cultures. Accordingly, leader-member relations are good in both cultures.

The central tenet of the LMX is that leaders do not treat each subordinate the same. This is the very essence of leadership both *by* and *with* diversity. Cultural intelligence is therefore very important even if only it is to be aware that when it comes to task performance, building commitment and making transformations, the leadership has to be of good quality in *all* cultures. The old adage "think global, act local" still applies but at least there are three aspects of leadership which appear to increase team performance *globally*. Meanwhile, leaders also have to act locally...

LEVERAGING DIVERSITY

Put simply, diversity is a source of creativity. Without it organisations are going to struggle to innovate and adapt in an increasingly fast-paced and ever-changing world. So says Groysberg and Connolly in the article "Great Leaders Who Make the Mix Work", HBR, Sept 2013. From interviewing the CEOs of global companies that had a reputation for "inclusiveness" they concluded that advancing diversity was a business imperative (staying competitive) and a moral imperative (value-driven). So how is diversity leveraged within an organisation? The answer lies in moving from "diversity" to "inclusivity": diversity is about the mix of people; inclusiveness is about making that mix work. Here are the practices which have been the most effective at "harnessing" diversity:

LEVERAGING DIVERSITY

Of the 24 companies that had most successfully leveraged diversity (measured by employment statistics, leadership attitudes and third-party recognition), the CEOs cited the following 8 practices as the most effective in leveraging diversity:

Measure Diversity

What gets measured gets done. This is not just about diversity targets; this is about inclusion sentiment that can usually be measured through employee engagement surveys.

Hold Managers Accountable

Not just about numbers, this is about actions. Each manager should be able to demonstrate that they have done something to leverage diversity (e.g. mentoring, training, sponsoring events).

Support Flexible Work Arrangements

For both males and females, balancing personal and professional commitments was considered the biggest barrier to diversity. Flexible hours and working-from-home can help break this barrier.

Recruit and Promote from Diverse Pools of Talent

Not just at the entry level; promote diversity from within otherwise senior diversity will never change. Extend quota systems to ensure a diverse pool of candidates to choose from for any post.

Provide Leadership Education

Not just at senior levels, leaders should be developed at junior levels where there is generally more diversity.

Diversity training should be for the "norm-group"; not just for the "diversity".

Sponsor Employee Resource Groups and Mentoring Programs

With a senior business sponsor, resource groups can provide structured professional development opportunities e.g. internal think-tanks and mentoring programs for affiliation groups.

Offer Quality Role Models

Diversity at the top promotes diversity throughout the organisation. One thing is the "talk" but it needs to be seen to be "walked" at the very highest levels.

Make the Chief Diversity Officer Position Count

A "CDO" position "institutionalizes the process and the intent." Once formalized, it can be the anchor to develop metrics and subsequent follow-up (see point #1...).

Some leaders remain undecided about the merits of diversity. Ironically, this can be because the diversity is present in the organisation but it is not yet considered to be "delivering". Leaders would be right to reflect on their own moral imperative for diversity and their particular business imperative relative to their project; however "diversity" cannot be relied on to "deliver" on its own – leaders cannot stand back and ask diversity to "prove" itself since this will set a new standard for measuring diversity i.e. do the "diverse" talent deliver as good as or better than the "majority" or "norm-group" talent? In such a case, not only is diversity not leveraged but this puts a barrier in place since to "prove" themselves, diverse talent would have to assimilate into the "norm-group" culture thereby losing all the benefits of diversity! Diversity should be included so that all talent can deliver to their maximum potential whilst remaining authentic (and not being measured by "norm-group" references). In short, if a leader is open to diversity, there is a chance that it will succeed; if however the leader is sceptical about diversity, the outcome is already known! In the context of the above 8 steps, it all starts with the leaders' attitudes...

LEADING DIVERSE TEAMS

How do you lead diverse teams? This can be a very difficult question to answer and one which is often overlooked, or even ignored by the team leader. In fact, team member diversity itself might not derail the team in the pursuit of its objectives, especially if the level of diversity in the team is either very high or very low; however anything in-between can pose significant challenges for the leader. This is the central theory of an article by Gratton et al, 2007, "Bridging Faultlines in Diverse Teams", MIT Sloan Management Review.

Their theory is that strong "faultlines" emerge in a team where there are a few fairly homogenous subgroups that are able to identify themselves on either a surface level (such as gender, age, nationality) or on a "deeper" level (such as values, personality and knowledge). When there are distinct non-overlapping categories, "faultlines" can become very strong e.g. a team made up of women under 30 years old and men over 50. Faultlines emerge when the team gets to know each other's' similarities and differences and can ultimately inhibit the exchange of knowledge and impede the team's creative and innovative capacity. Here's how to tackle faultlines and lead a diverse team:

LEADING DIVERSE TEAMS

Diagnose the probability of faultlines emerging

It is important to note that faultlines are not a natural result of diversity *per se*, but are found in situations of moderate diversity, when a team is neither very homogenous nor very heterogeneous in member attributes.

Focus on Task Orientation when a team is newly formed

The natural inclination of leaders to overcome the risk of emerging faultlines is to focus on relationships; however this can exacerbate the problem in the early stages of the team formation. Focusing on the task in the early stages can overcome this.

Later switch to Relationship Orientation

Whilst being task oriented in the early stages can increase team effectiveness, the "deeper" faultlines will eventually emerge. These can only be addressed by relationship orientation which is vital to ensure longer term team effectiveness.

The rhetorical question that the authors pose themselves is "how does a team leader know when to switch from task to relationship orientation"? They suggest that the switch will only be "successful at the point at which the team has sufficient shared experience to have developed a clear protocol for communication and coordination of activities and an established operational structure." An interpretation of this might be at that point when the team: 1. clearly knows the expectations of the project; 2. have clearly defined roles and tasks; and 3. are communicating regularly in a constructive manner. The authors state that leaders need to be able to answer themselves the question as to when to make the switch based on their team's needs and characteristics (i.e. it is case specific).

The interesting point for many multinational companies is that faultlines are mostly found where there is "moderate" diversity. It almost appears paradoxical that full diversity might be easier to manage than partial diversity; however if that is the case and given that some diversity is inevitable, then more diversity must be the only solution! Notwithstanding the team members, consider the situation if the majority of team leaders originate from a "fairly homogenous subgroup" having the same education, nationality, approximate age and gender! As the authors state, knowledge transfer can be greatly inhibited along with creativity and innovation. Diversity should therefore not only be considered on a team-by-team basis but on an organization basis including reference to the leaders themselves!

LEADING TEMPORARY TEAMS

s there a difference between leading a temporary team rather than a permanent team? Not just a question of timing, temporary teams are now often multi-disciplinary, multi-cultural and multi-locational; in other words there are many challenges to leading this particular type of team. In Amy Edmondson's Harvard Business Review article, "Teamwork on the Fly", April 2012, instead of seeing temporary teams as a problem, she sees them as a solution as to how companies can adapt to an ever-changing world; and potentially as a solution to bridging different national, organizational and occupational cultures. The author states that "in today's fast-moving, ultracompetitive global business environment, you can't rely on stable teams to get the work done. Instead, you need 'teaming'". Here's how 'teaming' is best achieved:

LEADING TEMPORARY TEAMS

The author proposes that several project management principles (scoping, structuring and sorting) help leaders facilitate effective 'teaming'; and cross-boundary collaboration can be achieved with leadership skills (emphasizing purpose, building psychological safety and embracing failure and conflict). Here's the summary:

Scoping
Scope the challenge, determine the expertise and clearly outline roles and responsibilities. This includes continually articulating the best possible current definition of the work.

Structuring
Boundaries and targets need to be established along with teamwork tools (conference and webinar communications, chat rooms, internet site and shareware).

Sorting
Reciprocal interdependence (as opposed to sequential) is required with back-and-forth (almost constant) team communication in order to mutually adjust according to progress.

Emphasizing Purpose
Articulating purpose is always important but even more so in a temporary team. Answering why the project exists is fundamental and can "galvanize even the most diverse, amorphous team".

Building Psychological Safety
To encourage the sharing of information, leaders must

exemplify a safe environment by exhibiting their own weaknesses and acknowledging ignorance where appropriate.

Embracing Failure and Conflict

Rather than avoiding them, accept and learn from failures! With conflict, reflection takes less time than fighting: replace advocacy (explaining and teaching) with inquiry (curiosity and listening).

The author states that "'teaming' can help to change a culture from localized hierarchical decision making to horizontal collaboration" (as demonstrated in Danone with 'teaming' known as "Networking Attitude"); however it is also arguable that some corporate cultures might more easily accommodate 'teaming' than others. Trompenaars defines four different corporate cultures according to the level of formality and centralization. Centralized cultures might not readily accept 'teaming', namely informal/centralized (the "family"); and formal/centralized (the "Eiffel Tower"). Decentralized corporate cultures where 'teaming' might prevail are informal/decentralized (the "incubator"); and formal/decentralized (the "guided missile") which is similar to what other commentators call an "adhocracy" where teams come together temporarily to achieve common tasks... Nevertheless, the author's principle argument is that with the rapidly changing world, 'teaming' is becoming more and more important and by implication, some corporate cultures might need to become less centralized.

The author cites conflict as a great source of creativity, but investment has to be made both in the team and beyond the team to ensure that cultural diversity does not in itself become a conflict. For example, for one of the 'teaming' projects, "the project leaders facilitated the successful outcome by assigning those rare specialists who had deep familiarity with both Chinese and Western culture to spend time in each other's firms helping to bridge differences in language, norms, practices and expectations." Multi-cultural, multi-locational teams might therefore be better comprised of individuals who have already been expatriated. One of the key points from the article – inquiry rather than advocacy – could be equally applied to all inter-cultural relations. Otherwise, leading a permanent team is reasonably similar to leading a temporary team. Notwithstanding the added urgency with a temporary team to define scope and purpose, implement structure and safety, the key difference in terms of leadership for a temporary global team is the need for the leader to be culturally sensitive.

GLOBAL COMMUNICATION

"The command and control approach to management has in recent years become less and less viable. Globalisation, new technologies, and changes in how companies create value and interact with customers have sharply reduced the efficacy of a purely top-down model of leadership." This is according to Groysberg and Slind in their article "Leadership is a Conversation: How to improve employee engagement and alignment in today's flatter, more networked organisations", June 2012, Harvard Business Review.

Their central argument is that leadership should be a dialogue rather than a monologue. Whilst this presents a challenge for the "old corporate" model of leadership communication, it is now also an opportunity in the "new organisational" model. Due to technical advances, there are more means available to have these conversations; however the new leader has to be more engaging with staff because the new technology blurs the frontier between the organisation and the public. Here's how to move from the old style to the new style of communicating globally:

GLOBAL COMMUNICATION

The authors suggest that there are four main elements of organisational "conversations" with each having implications as to how the leader should communicate:

Intimacy (how leaders relate to employees)

Whereas in the old corporation, information was primarily top-down and formal;

... in the new organisation, leaders communicate personally and directly. Informal, leaders place emphasis on trust and authenticity.

Interactivity (how leaders trust communication channels)

Whereas in the old corporation, messages were broadcast with a predominance of newsletters, memos and speeches;

... in the new organisation, leaders talk with employees not to them, with an emphasis on face-to-face dialogue.

Inclusion (how leaders develop organisational content)

Whereas in the old corporation, top executives controlled messaging and employees were "passive" consumers of information;

... in the new organisation, leaders emphasise content over control and employees become "active" consumers of information.

<u>**Intentionality (how leaders convey strategy)**</u>
Whereas in the old corporation, communication was fragmented, reactive and ad-hoc with leaders using "assertion" to achieve strategic alignment;

... in the new organisation, leaders have a clear over-arching agenda which is clearly explained to employees and strategy starts to evolve in a bottom-up fashion.

There may be many leaders who find themselves in an "old corporation" but wish to be in a "new organisation". Making the change from the old to the new could take time as this would be a cultural change. There is however the possibility for any leader becoming the bridge between two worlds: above, the old corporation; below, the new organisation. The "transitionary" leader who wishes to change the culture would for some time have to maintain the challenging position of effectively balancing both styles of communication...

5. LEADERSHIP AND: CHANGING *THE* WORLD

By now you will be ready to learn how to lead changes! First considering creativity, this section then looks at innovation and in particular how to overcome common barriers to innovation. To effect change the leader needs to know about effective decision-making processes and decision biases. These are considered before turning how to "sell" your change project, how to lead changes and finally how to accelerate change. In reaching this stage you will have completed your leadership development journey from *the* changing world to changing *the* world.

CREATIVITY AND LEADERSHIP

In a changing world where organizations need to innovate quicker than the competition in order to survive, the leaders first have to find the creative "spark" to "fire" the innovation. Creativity is however very difficult to manage; indeed many leaders consider it too elusive and intangible to be managed. So says Amabile et al., in their October 2008 HBR article "Creativity and the role of the leader". Following a Harvard Business School colloquium on the subject, the authors summarize that "you can't manage creativity, but you can manage for creativity." In order to enhance organizational creativity, leaders should therefore consider three key practices. Here's how:

CREATIVITY AND LEADERSHIP

The recommendations for leaders to foster the conditions in which creativity flourish are as follows:

Elicit ideas from all ranks
Stop thinking that you have the best ideas; most of the best ideas come from the "ranks".

Make it safe to fail: stress the goal is to experiment constantly, and learn early from failure.

Motivate people by giving positive feedback, asking questions and encouraging the team.

Open up to diverse perspectives
Recruit and develop diverse staff: diversity enhances creativity.

Get people of different disciplines, backgrounds and expertise to share their thinking.

Avoid suppressing all or parts of people's identity.

Correctly impose controls
Don't impose controls during the "discovery" phase of ideas. Brainstorm openly.

Protect those doing creative work from conformist forces within the organization.

Create a filtering mechanism in the commercial phase, possibly using third parties.

An engineering professor at this colloquium noted that most companies have hierarchical structures and differences in status among people impede the exchange of ideas. If the hierarchy is maintained but leaders want to overcome this challenge (and implement the above practices), the same professor suggested two further solutions:

1/ in the longer term, the reward system has to be changed: those who are rewarded should be those who help others succeed; and 2/ in the immediate, management's mission should be to get people to "shut up" and listen when appropriate. Indeed with the demands of day-to-day management and exigencies of operational excellence, talent development and listening are often overlooked...

LEADERSHIP AND INNOVATION

On the premise that innovation is a necessity just to survive, many organisations pose the question, "how" can we innovate? In particular, organisations might look to their leaders to achieve innovation. Breaking silos, bringing people together, sponsoring and effecting change, nurturing creativity, developing talent and leveraging diversity are all things that you might expect from a leader which might also contribute to innovation. But is there a direct link between leadership and innovation?

To answer that, it can be seen from a slightly different perspective that if leadership is not done well, innovation might "suffer" as a consequence. This angle was elaborated on in article by F. Vermeulen in the Business Strategy Review (London Business School, 2011, Vol 22, No 4) which highlighted "Five Mistaken Beliefs Business Leaders Have about Innovation". The case in point is that even though innovation has been looked at from "every conceivable" angle, the same leadership mistakes are often repeated which "hamper rather than induce" innovation. Here's a summary:

LEADERSHIP AND INNOVATION

Mistaken beliefs leaders have about innovation:

Believing the numbers

The mistake is to insist on the "numbers" (e.g. market size, NPV etc).

… If something is truly innovative, it is impossible to reliably produce numbers

Believing success has been attained

The mistake is the "success trap" – believing success is permanent and ignoring innovation.

… The business context also changes and continuing adaptation is needed to survive

Believing they know the competition

The mistake is to think that similar companies are the most important competitors.

… The most "threatening" innovation often comes from an "adjacent" angle

Believing that because it's always been done this way, then "this" is the best way

The mistake it to keep doing things as before even when circumstances change.

… The greatest innovations often come from challenging industry conventions

> ## Believing the customer
> The mistake is to think that consumer research is useful for truly innovative ideas.
>
> … If you want to be really innovative, you have to be leading the customers

It appears that the leaders can do a lot to "kill" innovation just by resorting to classic "management" behaviours. The first point to note regarding leadership and innovation is that leaders should be well connected with the outside world and not just focused on their product, their business and their organisation. Imagine doing a simple "Strengths, Weaknesses, Opportunities, Threats" analysis with only an internal perspective – it is likely that the result would focus mainly on the strengths! Secondly, by looking outside the organisation, leaders can make sure the organisation is at least adaptive. Finally, there has to be a corporate culture which "permits" innovation: leaders have to tolerate failure.

OVERCOMING ORGANISATIONAL RIGIDITIES

Claudio Feser, an executive at McKinsey consulting, started researching corporate longevity and found that 50% of all publically listed companies die within 10 years; only 15% reach 30 years; and only 5% achieve their 50th anniversary. Further research focused on this 5% whom he referred to as "serial innovators" – those who were continually able to adapt and change in order to survive. In his book, "Serial Innovators: Firms that Change the World" (John Wiley & Sons, 2011) he identifies organisational rigidities that can lead to the demise of most firms and also details how the "serial innovators" overcome these rigidities in order to change, grow and prosper.

Here's a summary of how to overcome organisational rigidities:

OVERCOMING ORGANISATIONAL RIGIDITIES

As companies age, they develop rigidities which block them from changing and adapting. Managers therefore need to overcome the following five rigidities:

---

1. Hierarchical Bureaucracy

Whilst hierarchical organisations can have their merits, ossification can take place when the organisation turns into a bureaucracy. Symptoms may include centralisation of decisions with little delegation of responsibility and "excess layers of management that slow their operations."

To create an "adaptive organisation" 1/ "positively frame the vision" seeing the future in an optimistic way whilst dealing with the issues of today; and 2/ carve out separate and autonomous units which can become "self-managed performance cells."

2. Loss of purpose

When companies become rigidly mired in the past, "paralysed [and] blind to the changes necessary to survive" then a sense of purpose can be lost. Without a sense of purpose, staff lose their sense of belonging along with their drive to achieve.

"Cultivate the desire to make a difference" – fulfill people's yearning to give to a greater cause and serve all stakeholders as well as the shareholders. Use motivational stories to engage staff and include altruistic objectives in the firm's mission.

3. Change-resistant corporate culture

After a certain time it is not just the rules and regulations that define what can and cannot be done but also the corporate culture. Whilst a strong culture can be beneficial if it is strategically aligned and adaptive, it can otherwise cause a change-resistant rigidity.

"Cultivate a culture that fosters execution" – promote values and "norms" that encourage achievement, along with creativity and new ways of thinking. When changes are proposed, instead of asking the question "why?" start asking the question "why not?"

4. Poor incentives

Purely monetary incentives can act as a rigidity as they tend to neither inspire nor retain staff for the long-term. Monetary rewards can "deter staff from cooperating, undermine 'moral behaviour' and even encourage deceit."

Balance financial and non-financial rewards and invest in staff development. Non-financial rewards need to be managed positively and visibly. Motivation can be increased through social recognition and performance feedback.

5. Adherence to the status quo

Some firms have "defining capabilities" in operations, abilities or specific assets; however these advantages can become restraints by tying the firm to the past and fossilising a "status quo". This limits the firm's ability to react to both opportunities and threats.

Two steps are required to overcome this: 1/ top executives need to have a strong desire to learn and "share diverse philosophical approaches"; and 2/ "invest in capabilities" – adapt readily to the pursuit of opportunities and have strategies in place to add to core competencies.

The author appears to presuppose that the readers have the power to make sweeping organisational changes and accordingly, at first glance, some of the advice might appear to be "easier said than done"! So what do you do if, as a middle manager, you find yourself in a rigid organisation? Firstly you can positively frame your own vision for your own followers and you can also protect them from the worst "excesses" of the "hierarchical bureaucracy" by fully empowering them: make them a "self-managed performance cell"! Secondly, with all the other rigidities, adopt the same approach: make a clear distinction between today and tomorrow and focus your followers on the tomorrow you wish to create: communicate a motivating sense of purpose; ask "why not?" rather than "why?"; develop your staff through feedback, coaching and training; never stop learning, promote diversity in all its forms and keep an eye on the opportunities and threats arising outside the organisation. You don't actually have to be the CEO to do this: you can start today!

LEADERSHIP AND DECISION MAKING

Decision-making is fundamental to leadership and the essence of change management: reviewing proposals and directing resources are all aspects of leadership and decision making. So how do you best make decisions as a leader? The answer depends on where you are in your career in terms of leadership: "senior", "mid" or "entry" level and whether those decisions are made in public or in private. This is according to Brousseau, Driver, Hourihan and Larsson in their 2006 article, "The Seasoned Executive's Decision-Making Style", Harvard Business Review.

According to their research, approaches to decision making differ in two ways: the use of information ("satisficing" with little information or "maximizing" with more information); and the number of options generated ("single focus" with one option and "multifocus" with many options). Mapping these two axes yields four decision-making styles. Further, people appear to use different styles in public (the "leadership style") than they do in private (the "thinking style") and the most appropriate styles to use evolve according to leadership seniority. Here's a summary of the four styles and the evolution:

LEADERSHIP AND DECISION MAKING

There are four styles of decision-making:

Decisive (little information, one option)

The private thinking style is direct, efficient, fast and firm

The public leadership style is action-focused and comes across as task-orientated

Flexible (little information, many options)

The private thinking style is about speed and adaptability

The public leadership style comes across as social and responsive

Hierarchic (more information, one option)

The private thinking style is highly analytical and considered "final"

The public leadership style is complex and highly intellectual

Integrative (more information, many options)

The private thinking style is broad and uses many inputs for many solutions

The public leadership style is creative and highly participative

These styles show a particular evolution over the course of a leader's development:

<u>For public leadership</u>, the most appropriate decision-making style at "entry" level is "decisive" whereas the least applicable is "flexible". At the "mid" level these start to inverse and temporarily equate with the other two styles. At "senior" level, the most appropriate decision-making style is "flexible" (whereas "decisive" is relegated to last place).

<u>For private thinking</u>, the most appropriate decision-making style at "entry" level is "flexible" whereas the least applicable is "integrative". At the "mid" level these start to inverse and temporarily equate with the other two styles. At "senior" level, the most appropriate decision-making style is "integrative" (whereas "flexible" is relegated to last place).

How you decide in public and private appear to be diametrically opposed; however this is not irrational. For a first-line supervisor, minimal information and a single option is appropriate for "decisively" leading task-orientated decisions "on the shop floor". Nevertheless, in private, the "entry" level leader is actually "flexibly" thinking about various different options, even though reviewing lots of information might not be possible. For a "senior" leader, the accent is on flexibility in public – leading with options from little information. At the same time, the leader needs to think in an "integrative" manner to consider both more options and obtain as much information as possible.

According to the research of 120,000 individuals the hierarchical style never appears to be the most or least appropriate leading or thinking style. For both public and private decision making, the hierarchical style has mid-range prevalence at the "entry" level which then dips at the "mid" level before recovering to a higher prevalence at the "senior" level. Only amongst Europeans and only in private for thinking decisions did the hierarchical style prove successful at a "senior" level (above "integration"). What is interesting is that otherwise, having reviewed the results regionally, (Asia, North America, Latin America and Europe), these evolutions in both leadership and thinking decision-making styles "follow the same trajectory across all four continents".

This has some implications for leadership development:

1. If all leaders start their career thinking flexibly, they should then develop and adapt this style later in their career into the public space to lead flexibly (more options even with little information).

2. Decisiveness has its moment early in a leader's career but becomes less significant (both privately and publically) later.

3. Unless in Europe and in private and then only at senior level, the hierarchical style should be used with care!

4. For private decision making, the art of the "integrative" decision style should be developed: at senior level, seek more information to make more options – look outside and beyond your normal frame of reference!

MINIMISING DECISION-MAKING BIASES

Managers like to think that the decisions they make are objective and rational and have been executed taking into consideration all the pertinent facts. In reality, many other forces come into play when making a decision such that most decisions are usually subjective, irrational and have been made with only limited information. As Wolf explains in his HBR blog post of September 2012, "How to minimise your biases when making decisions", it is mainly inherent biases which cause decisions to be sub-optimal. Accordingly, in order to optimise decisions, biases have to be recognised and then minimised. Here's a summary of decision-making biases and how to overcome them:

MINIMISING DECISION-MAKING BIASES

Drawing on studies from Rosenzweig, Kahneman and Schoemaker, there are six principle decision-making biases noted as follows:

Anchoring

If expecting the same outcome as before, contradictory data tends to be ignored or omitted. This becomes

---

more acute with numbers which are difficult to "adjust away" from.

To overcome anchoring, "seek diverse outside opinion to counter overconfidence".

Framing
How a situation is presented affects the decision. In addition and generally, the pain of losing is perceived to be more powerful than the pleasure of winning.

To overcome framing, inverse the perspective from positive to negative or *vice versa*.

Availability Heuristic
Vivid and easily imaginable events (even if uncommon) along with recent events are weighted disproportionately higher than unimaginable or past events.

To overcome availability heuristic, "search relentlessly for potentially relevant or disconfirming evidence".

Confirmation Bias
Initial decisions become self-fulfilling prophecies. Data is collected after the event to justify the decision (similar to anchoring).

To overcome confirmation bias, accept a "chief contrarian" as part of the team.

Commitment Escalation

It is difficult to accept "failure" and start again from scratch; instead, previous commitments tend to influence current decisions.

To overcome commitment escalation, ignore the old problem by clearly redefining the new problem.

Hindsight Bias

Once something is known, it is difficult to remember when it was not known. This can make it more difficult to learn from failures (as it is now "obvious").

To overcome hindsight bias, reward due process (and in particular "lessons learnt") rather than penalising failure.

The above decision-making biases are compiled at the individual level but despite the best efforts of any individual, decision-making biases can easily become "institutionalised" in an organisation. All of the biases noted above can reinforce organisational culture: for example, it would be a very brave individual who could go to the board of Kodak in the early 1990s and tell them that photographic film was doomed and they should start preparing for an exit (yet look what happened)! To optimise the decision-making process and overcome decision-making biases, make sure the team making the decision is diverse! The process might seem to be more "painful" but the end-result should be a higher quality decision!

LEADERSHIP AND BUY-IN

Many authors have associated leadership with making changes, but no leader can effect a change without having first "sold" their idea to the key stakeholders. Kotter has argued that a lack of communication before, during and after the change is a common theme in the failure of change management projects. Focusing on the communication both before and during the change, he recently published a book with LA Whitehead entitled "Buy-in: saving your good idea from getting shot down" (2010). Here's a summary of how leaders ensure "buy-in":

LEADERSHIP AND BUY-IN

Instead of Q&A, the authors speak of A&R: "Attacks" that any idea for change is likely to encounter along with generic "Responses". Twelve proposed A&R can be categorised as follows:

Problem Denial

A – We've been successful so far so why change?

R – Success is temporary and to succeed further we must adapt.

A – You imply that we have been failing!

R – No, we suggest we have been doing a good job within the current limitations.

Solution Denial

A – What about this, and that, and this, and that...?

R – All good new ideas eventually raise questions which cannot be answered.

A – You are abandoning our core values!

R – The plan and the accompanying change actually uphold our core values!

A – No one else does this!

R – Do your homework or prove that you are the very first!

A – We tried it before and it did not work.

R – That was then. Conditions and context have now changed.

Implementation Denial

A – Good idea, but this is not the right time.

R – The best time is now and this is urgent, because...

A – It's just too much work to do this!

R – A real challenge is a good challenge and this is a priority because…

A – It won't work here; we're different.

R – Relative to this particular problem and solution, we are similar because…

A – It puts us on a slippery slope to disaster.

R – This change will not lead to disaster in any form because…

A – You'll never convince enough people.

R – That's almost never possible; but I would like you to be convinced because…

A – We are simply not equipped to do this.

R – We already have much of what we need and we can get the rest because…

Some readers might liken the above generic responses to Schopenhauer's "The art of being right: 38 ways to win an argument", however, here, it is meant to be a sales technique to ensure buy-in rather than anything more intellectual, manipulative or even Machiavellian. Indeed, the real key to success is to have done your homework before making your pitch. What is interesting in the above categorisation is that the "implementation denials" really have to be supported with specific facts in addition to the generic response. It is also interesting to note that it might be better to spend more time on the solution than the problem and more time again on the implementation plan!

It should however be noted that the "buy-in" is only half the journey. Once sold, the change project actually has to be achieved (and continually communicated). In organisations with very strong and formal hierarchies, the "effecting change" part of the equation can often be overlooked! The "buy-in" is key and once approved by the "top," the change implementation is sometimes neglected on the false premise that since it carries the badge of most-senior approval it can be implemented by simple "command". Worse, when this approach becomes part of the corporate culture, too much time can be spent doing homework and getting everything impeccably correct before approval is sought. That can kill innovation and slow down the organisation's adaption with the changing environment: ultimately, it can impede the competitive advantage of the organisation.

LEADING CHANGES BY NETWORKING

What does a leader needs to make innovation happen in a large organization? A keyword which often figures in any review is networking: both to receive information so as to assess what "can" be done (rather than what might be done); and then to influence others to make changes happen even when faced with uncertainty. What type of network might be best for a leader to effect innovation and/or make changes? According to Battilana *et al.*, "it depends", but in their HBR article the authors give clear guidance as to what network types can improve the leader's chance of innovating: "The Network Secrets of Great Change Agents" (July 2013). Here's how to lead changes by networking:

LEADING CHANGES BY NETWORKING

The authors focused their research on finding effective change agents in large organizations and then mapping their success to the type and nature of the network they had. The predictors of the change agents' success were the following:

136

Central

Change agents who are central in their organization's informal network "have a clear advantage", regardless of their position in the formal hierarchy.Review your network.

If you are not central (like a "hub" with many "spokes" spanning 360°), either develop your network and/or engage someone who is in order to achieve the change.

Bridge (for Dramatic Changes)

When the person's network contacts are not connected to each other, the person makes the bridge between disparate individuals and groups. This proves best for making "dramatic" changes.

If you are proposing divergent change which disrupts existing practices then make sure your network is a "bridging" type or "appoint a co-chair whose relation-ships offer a better fit".

Cohesion (for Minor Changes)

When the person's network is cohesive (i.e. contacts are also connected to each other), the ease of facilitating communication and building trust proves ideal for mak-ing "minor" changes.

Once the change proposal is "out", a cohesive network either tends to fully cooperate or to form a coalition against the change; hence the suitability for minor rather than dramatic changes.

Closeness to other influencers

Defining closeness in terms of "mutual trust, liking and a sense of social obligation", being close to "change endorsers" proved to have no impact on the success of either dramatic or minor changes; but being close to "fence-sitters" had high impact on the success of either type of change.

Being close to "change resistors" impacted success for minor changes; however closeness had no impact on the success of dramatic changes (since when resistors perceive a significant threat they are typically difficult to influence otherwise).

So it really does depend! Innovation comes in many shapes and forms from incremental adaptive changes to large and singular disruptions. These changes can be best managed according to the type of network the leader has; however if we change the frame of reference from "network" to "ecosystem" then the position of the leader in the "eco-system" is by no means leader-centric! The leader is part of a larger ecosystem and will accordingly have to adapt to the environment which might be impacted by the local culture (national or organizational). Some cultures might be collegiate and group-orientated whereas others might be competitive and individual-focused. The former might lend itself to "cohesive" networks; the latter to "bridging" networks. Therefore in turn, and despite the best efforts of the leader, in collegiate and group-orientated cultures, innovation and change might only occur on an incremental, gradual and "minor" basis; whereas in competitive and individual-focused cultures, innovation and change might happen more often as large and singular disruptions!

LEADING CHANGE

In a report by the Conference Board think-tank, "Strategic Leadership Development: Global Trends and Approaches", in excess of 650 HR professionals were asked in 2012 what are the most important leadership characteristics 1) ranking most important now; 2) which are developed in leadership programs; and 3) which are the most important over the next five years. The number one answer to all those three questions was "leading change". Unequivocally, across regions, nationalities, cultures and industries, leading change is *the* most important. So how do you lead change? One of the best tools for leaders to reference is Berenschot's "Seven Forces Model" (1991). Here's how to lead change:

LEADING CHANGE

Unlike Kotter's eight steps model (1990) which focuses on why and how changes can fail, Berenschot's change model focuses on the forces which make change happen. Of the seven, the first three are "stories" which the leader communicates, the fourth is the "fuel" that the leader provides for the other forces and the last three are the "actions" that the leader needs to initiate.

Necessity

This usually has to be a shock to break the inertia and to create a sense of urgency.

Necessity "moves" and usually sparks a sense of "being in this together".

Vision

The leader envisions the changes for other to see what is requested of them.

Vision "directs" by inspiring others and creating a sense of purpose.

Success

To convince followers there must be early proof to confirm that the change is possible.

Success "makes believe" that the new way is better.

Spirit

The leader's strength to not only initiate but maintain a high level of engagement.

Spirit is how the leader "gives power" to the other forces.

Structure

Structural support at organizational level to challenge people and to endorse changes.

Structures "challenge" the current way of working and then support the proposed change.

Capabilities
Knowledge, skills and empowerment to achieve the new tasks.

Capabilities "make possible" the changes by providing the necessary resources.

Systems
Information, reviews and feedback to confirm the desired performance (skills and behaviours).

Systems "reinforce" the change both during the implementation and after.

Leading change takes a lot of energy and a lot of force! One can consider that there are four initial responses to a proposed change: 1/ Resistant – will pro-actively block the change; 2/ Neutral – either for or against the change but will not actively participate in the change process; 3/ Reluctant – for the change but will actively avoid participation in the change process; and 4/ Positive – is for the change and will proactively support the change effort. Only the last one out of those four positions will provide their own "force" to the change and that is after the leader has highlighted the necessity, communicated the vision and even demonstrated some early proofs! This is why the leader needs "spirit" to bring (at least) those who are 'reluctant' and 'neutral' "on board" and then go the extra mile to effect the "actions". To be capable of leading change, you need to therefore align your passion, your talent and your opportunity!

HOW LEADERS ACCELERATE CHANGE

Kotter in his article "Accelerate!" HBR, November 2012, draws on his own "leading change" material along with that of Porter, Christensen and Kahneman to propose a solution to the dilemma that companies today "must constantly seek competitive advantage without disrupting daily operations". His theory is that traditional hierarchies and managerial processes are very good at addressing the daily demands of running a company; however "what they do not do well is identify the most important hazards and opportunities early enough, formulate creative strategic initiatives nimbly enough, and implement them fast enough". He therefore proposes that two systems should operate in concert: one the "rational" hierarchy; the other a "more emotional" network. The latter is based on his eight-step change method but importantly, in the network, the steps become "accelerators".

The network ensures that the accelerators are current and always at work (rather than being used in a rigid and sequential way); and instead of change being driven by one small powerful group, the accelerators "pull in as many people as possible from throughout the organisation to form a 'volunteer army'". This network approach overcomes the two principal change resistors found in a hierarchy: 1/ political: managers being "loath to take chances without permission from their superiors"; and 2/ cultural: people "cling to their habits and fear loss of power and stature." Here's how to accelerate change:

HOW LEADERS ACCELERATE CHANGE

According to Kotter, "mounting complexity and rapid change create strategic challenges that even a souped-up hierarchy can't handle. That's why the dual operating system – a management-driven hierarchy working in concert with a strategic network – works so remarkably well". The dual operating system has five principles:

Many change agents, not just a few

To move "faster and further, you need to pull more people than ever into the strategic change game", but in a way that is economically feasible. 10% of managers and employees at any one time is proposed by Kotter as both "plenty and possible".

A "want-to" not just a "have-to" mindset

To mobilise a "voluntary army" people have to want to be change agents and must be given permission to do so. The spirit of volunteerism (the desire to work with others for a "shared purpose") "energises" the network.

Head and heart, not just head

In order to engage management and staff in the change network, you must "speak to their genuine desire to contribute to positive change and to take an enterprise in strategically smart ways into a better future, giving greater meaning and purpose to their work."

More leadership, not just more management

The hierarchy needs competent management; the strategy network needs lots of leadership. It's "all about vision, opportunity, agility, inspired action, and celebration – not project management, budget reviews, reporting relationships, compensation and accountability to a plan."

Two systems, one organisation

The dual operating system is not two silos: "the network and the hierarchy must be inseparable with a constant flow of information and activity between them – an approach that works in part because the volunteers in the network all work within the hierarchy."

It is quite possible that this "win-win" solution will become the defining hallmark of corporate strategic change initiatives from now on! Its simplicity is beguiling and it solves the ultimate change-management question: how to effect change without having to change the hierarchy itself! However, the idea of a hierarchy being staffed by managers whilst simultaneously super-motivated and highly-engaged leaders form volunteer armies with a sense of purpose to effect change highlights one key point which should not be overlooked: at least someone in the hierarchy (very near the top) must have sufficient leadership (and management) capabilities to introduce, promote and sponsor such a change-network! Without that initial "birth" of the network from the hierarchy, the hierarchy is at risk at remaining just that!

From a Human Resources point of view, what Kotter is proposing might be the new, modern and collective version of the now old-fashioned concept of individual "garage-time"? Hitherto, in an attempt to foster innovation, many companies permitted employees to spend 10-20% of their work time on individual projects on the understanding that any resulting innovations would become the property of the company. 3M had its famous "post-it" product succeed in such a way, but that is now an old story. Google recently revitalised the idea and coined the term "garage time" but insiders insist that it is no longer a genuine offer and publically the corporation no longer promotes it. When it was fashionable, it was billed as a key offer to attract, motivate and retain staff. Now perhaps organisations should offer collective "change time" for those willing to work together on strategic change initiatives?

Staying with HR, from a learning and development point of view, this is both a fantastic opportunity and a reflection of what already happens in many large organisations.

As part of a leadership development course, many corporate universities offer "action-learning" projects which in a way work exactly like Kotter's proposed "volunteer armies" not necessarily effecting change but at least studying and proposing change under the tutelage of a senior sponsor. Not only do the diverse leaders from all parts of the organisation come together and work in a team getting to learn about the challenges of change management and developing as leaders; but also, if the proposed projects are strategic in nature then the organisation itself can gain fast insight into the changes that are needed to maintain a competitive advantage without disrupting daily operations!

WAY FORWARD: WHILE YOU ARE LEADING CHANGES...

Post-development, you have to deliver and keep on delivering and so as an epilogue to your leadership development there are two more chapters: one on managing your energy to help you stay the course; and another on how to "stay on track" and avoid derailment.

MANAGE YOUR ENERGY, NOT YOUR TIME

Leaders often complain that there are not enough hours in the day to get everything done. A straightforward solution might be to reorganize, reprioritize, reschedule or otherwise better manage your time. That might be a short term solution, but for the longer term it might be better to try and manage your *energy*. This is the essence of an article originally published in October 2007 in the Harvard Business Review where Schwartz and McCarthy proposed how to "Manage Your Energy, Not Your Time". Time is a finite resource, but energy is different – here's what the authors say:

MANAGE YOUR ENERGY, NOT YOUR TIME

What can be done instead of reducing sleep, quality family time and even skipping meals? The authors suggest there are four domains where the focus can be on energy rather than time:

Physical energy

- Reduce stress by exercising: three times a week cardio; at least once a week strength.

- Eat small meals and regulate intake to every three hours; reduce alcohol consumption.
- Take brief but regular breaks during the day; go to bed earlier.

Emotional energy

- Fuel positive emotions by proactively engaging in positive feedback.
- Look at difficult situations through new "lenses". Reverse lens – what would the other person say (which might be right); long lens – how important will this be in six months; and wide lens – how can I grow and learn from this situation?

Mental energy

- Perform high-concentration tasks away from phones and email.
- Only respond to voice- and e-mails at designated times during the day.
- Every night identify the key point for the next day.

Spiritual energy

- Identify activities for which you have a passion; and then focus on these.

- Review what is most important to you and then focus on that.
- Identify and then live your core values.

For "physical" energy the recommendations are reasonably obvious but the trouble is that it always seems easier said than done! Seek a coach if you are finding difficulty with this. "Emotional" energy is interesting: firstly the focus on positive feedback – the more you give the better you feel; secondly, just taking a pause from the dynamic and looking at things through new lenses is a great way of assessing the situation objectively. Ask for help with this from friends and family outside work. "Mental" energy is something that is very challenging to manage at work in this era of instant everything, but a good tip is to only access email at pre-designated times during the day. In a sense, mental energy management is about knowing when to switch "on" (fully focus) and switch "off" (disconnect from work issues). For "spiritual" energy focusing on tasks which instil your passion is sound advice for a long and sustainable career!

LEADERSHIP DERAILMENT IN A GLOBAL CONTEXT

Derailment is defined as when talented or hitherto successful people fail to achieve their full potential. The research into leadership derailment usually focuses on the individual. Why did the leader fail to live up to expectations? What "went" wrong? What did they not do that they should have done and what did they do that they should not have done? It's usually all about the leader's behaviours whilst contextual and cultural considerations are often marginalised. Unfortunately for international executives working across borders in a global environment, there are potentially many more "derailers" than to be found "domestically". This is the opinion of McCall Jr. and Hollenbecks' "Developing Global Executives," Harvard Business School Press, 2002. Citing an "American" theory which from McCall's previous work where he studied why American executives derail in the USA, the authors then expand the research worldwide and see if the results are still valid in a global context.

LEADERSHIP DERAILMENT IN A GLOBAL CONTEXT

The authors describe four key dynamics which can derail leaders along with seven "universal fatal flaws" which are defined as "troublemakers".

Bad Timing

"A unique excellence becomes a fatal flaw". In other words the strengths that previously propelled the executive become weaknesses later on.

Overlooked Flaws

The executive was getting good results so flaws were tolerated up to a certain point beyond which they were no longer acceptable.

Arrogance

Hubris or wanton arrogance. Similar flaws include being overly ambitious or political along with an inability to listen.

Bad Luck

Wrong person in the wrong place at the wrong time. Even the most flawless executive is liable to this risk.

In amongst all these "dynamics" there are seven "universal fatal flaws" which cause "trouble":

1. Failure to learn or adapt to change

2. Bungled relationships with key people

3. Failure to take needed actions (and/or ask for help) to deliver on promises

4. Narrow or parochial perspective

5. Lack of people skills

6. Loss of contact with the rest of the company

7. Selecting a team of ineffective people

The authors applied the same research to see if this theory could be applied globally and their initial finding was that it could be. The same dynamics are prevalent in a global context and apply as equally to international executives overseas as to "domestic" executives at home. However, "while some global derailments were straightforward and the flaws obvious, many others were not". The authors conclude that besides the flaws of the individual and their actions (where the derailment dynamics still hold true), in a global context, the international executive is at risk of derailment due to two other forces: "Contextual Factors" and "Organisational Mistakes".

Contextual Factors start with the fact that the context is "significantly enriched in international settings by the added stress of a foreign environment and by differences in language, culture and belief systems that make inappropriate behaviour and misunderstandings more likely." If we consider that one of the keys to success is "fitting in" then it can be seen that this "rich" context is likely to increase the risk of derailment. The more complexities there are the more chance that something can go wrong. This is compounded with implicit cultures since the "hosts" might be reticent to give feedback whilst the "visitors" might find it impossible to read subtle clues. This is all the more reason to argue that the organisation should help and assist international executives on global assignments. This is something which, whilst not deliberate, is nevertheless avoidable and therefore noted by the authors as another derailment force: "Organisational Mistakes".

Organisational Mistakes include "the absence of feedback, little monitoring, the tolerance of existing flaws and a lack of support". Their study notes that the risk of organisational "negligence" can be particularly acute for foreign nationals coming to the company's headquarters and for executives returning home. The authors suggest that in the domestic arena, the company is only complicit in the derailment of the executive; whereas in a global context they are often the culprits. Sometimes support was implied but then not forthcoming when really needed; expectations were often unclear; feedback (if forthcoming) was seldom honest; and their home contacts often did not understand the local situation (or at worse did not care) and did not stay in contact unless problems arose.

For leaders operating globally there are a few key points to remember:

- Ensure you do not exhibit any of the "fatal flaws."

- Always remember that what got you where you are today might not be what will get you to where you want to go. Keep an eye on the dynamic and keep learning.

- Be aware that there is a higher risk of derailing internationally than domestically.

- As a leader in an organisation remember that you *are* the organisation. Do not assume that others will take care of the support for global executives: make sure you provide this support for your team and your organisation.

And finally…

- Refer back to this book as and when you need a reminder on how to *always* keep developing your leadership skills!

REFERENCES AND
FURTHER READING

T. M. Amabile & K. Mukti (2008), Harvard Business Review, "Creativity and the Role of the Leader."

K. Aquila, M. Dewhurst & S. Heywood (2012), McKinsey Quarterly, "Managing at a global scale."

N.J. Barger & L.K. Kirby (2004), "Introduction to Type and Change." CPP Inc.

T. Barta, M. Kleiner & T. Neumann (2012), McKinsey Quarterly, "Is there a payoff from top team diversity?"

F. Bartolomé and A. Laurent (1986), Harvard Business Review, "The Manager: master and servant of power."

J. Battilana & T. Casciaro (2013) Harvard Business Review, "The Network Secrets of Great Change Agents."

M. Brent & F. Elsa Dent, (2010), "The Leader's Guide to Influence: how to use soft skills to get hard results." Pearson Education.

K.R. Brousseau, M.J. Driver, G. Hourihan & R.Larsson (2006), Harvard Business Review, "The Seasoned Executive's Decision-Making Style."

M. Buckingham & C. Coffman (2005), "First Break all the Rules: what the world's greatest managers do differently." Pocket Books.

M. Buelens, H. Van Den Broeck, K. Vanderheyden, R. Kreitner & A. Kinicki (2006, 3rd ed.), "Organisational Behaviour." McGraw-Hill.

S. Cain (2012), "Quiet: the power of introverts in a world that can't stop talking." Crown.

K. Cameron & R. Quinn (1999), "Diagnosing and Changing Organizational Culture: based on the competing values framework." Addison-Wesley.

P. Cappelli (2008), Harvard Business Review, "Talent management for the twenty-first century."

R. Charan, S. Drotter & J. Noel (2011, 2nd ed.), "The Leadership Pipeline: how to build the leadership powered company." John Wiley & Sons.

R.B. Cialdini's (2006), "Influence: The Psychology of Persuasion." Collins Business Essentials.

J.A. Conger & R.M. Fulmer (2003), Harvard Business Review, "Developing your leadership pipeline."

J. Comfort & P. Franklin (2011), "The Mindful International Manager: how to work effectively across cultures." Kogan Page.

R. L. Cross, S. Parise & L. M. Weiss (2007), McKinsey Quarterly, "The role of networks in organisational change."

R. L. Cross, R. D. Martin & L. M. Weiss (2006), McKinsey Quarterly, "Mapping the value of employee collaboration."

A.P. De Geus (2004), "The Living Company: habits for survival in a turbulent business environment." Harvard Business School.

P. C. Early & E. Mosakowski (2004), Harvard Business Review, "Cultural Intelligence."

A. Edmondson (2012), Harvard Business Review, "Teamwork on the Fly."

C. Feser (2011), "Serial Innovators: firms that change the world." John Wiley & Sons.

C. Fernandez-Araoz, B. Groysberg & N. Nohria (2011), Harvard Business Review, "How to Hang on to Your High Potentials."

J. D. Ford & L. W. Ford (2009), Harvard Business Review, "Decoding Resistance to Change."

F. D. Frank, R.P. Finnegan, C.R. Taylor (2005), Human Resource Planning, "The race for talent: retaining and engaging workers in the 21st century."

R. M. Fulmer & J. A Conger (2004), "Growing your Company's Leaders: how great organisations use succession management to sustain competitive advantage." AMACOM.

B. George, P. Sims, A. McLean, D. Mayer (2007), Harvard Business Review, "Discovering your Authentic Leadership."

D. Goleman, R. Boyatzis & A. McKee (2002), "Primal Leadership: realising the power of emotions." Harvard Business School.

D. Goleman (2000), Harvard Business Review, "What Makes a Leader?"

D. Goleman (2000), Harvard Business Review, "Leadership That Gets Results."

L. Gratton, A. Voigt & T. Erickson (2007), MIT Sloan Management Review, "Bridging Faultlines in Diverse Teams."

K. Grint (2005), Human Relations, "Problems, problems, problems: the social construction of 'leadership'."

K. Grint (2008), Clinical Leader, "Wicked Problems and Clumsy Solutions."

B. Groysberg & M. Slind (2012), Harvard Business Review, "Leadership is a Conversation: how to improve employee engagement and alignment in today's flatter, more net-worked organisations."

B. Groysberg & K. Connolly (2013), Harvard Business Review, "Great Leaders Who Make the Mix Work."

M. Guthridge & A. B. Komm (2008), McKinsey Quarterly, "Why multinationals struggle to manage talent."

M. Guthridge, A.B. Komm & E. Lawson (2008), McKinsey Quarterly, "Making talent a strategic priority."

E. T. Hall & M. R. Hall (1990), "Understanding Cultural Differences: Germans, French and Americans." Nicholas Brealey.

S. ten Have, W. ten Have, F. Stevens, M. van der Elst & F. Pol-Coyne (2003), "Key Management Models: the management tools and practices that will improve your business." Pearson.

P. Hersey & H.B. Blanchard (2007, 9th ed.), "Management of Organisational Behaviour." Prentice Hall.

T. Hindle (2003, 2nd ed.), "Guide to management ideas." Economist Books.

G. Hofstede, G.J. Hofstede & M. Minkov (2010, 3rd ed.), "Cultures and Organizations: software of the mind." McGraw-Hill.

J. P. Kotter (2007), Harvard Business Review, "Leading Change: why transformation efforts fail."

J.P. Kotter (1990), Harvard Business Review, "What Leaders Really Do."

J.P. Kotter & J.L. Heskett (1992), "Corporate Culture and Performance." The Free Press.

J.P. Kotter & L.A. Whitehead (2010), "Buy-in: saving your good idea from being shot down." Harvard Business Review Press.

A. Laurent (1986), Human Resource Management, "Cross Cultural Puzzle of International Human Resource Management".

R. Lewis (2007, 2nd ed.), "The Cultural Imperative: global trends in the 21st century." Nicholas Brealey.

R. Lewis (2006, 2nd ed.), "When Cultures Collide: leading across cultures." Nicholas Brealey.

D. Livermore (2010), "Leading with Cultural Intelligence: the new secret to success." AMACOM.

J. Maxwell (2011), "The 5 Levels of Leadership: proven steps to maximize your potential." Hachette.

H. Mintzberg (1990, reprint), Harvard Business Review, "The Manager's job: folklore and fact."

R.T. Moran, P.R. Harris & S.V. Moran (2007, 7th ed.), "Managing Cultural Differences: global leadership strategies for the 21st century." Elsevier.

M.W. McCall Jr. (1998), "High Flyers: developing the next generation of leaders." Harvard Business School.

M.W. McCall Jr. & G.P. Hollenbeck, (2002), "Developing Global Executives: the lessons of international experience." Harvard Business School.

R.R. McCrae, A. Terracciano *et al.* (2005), Journal of Personality and Social Psychology, "Personality Profiles of Cultures: aggregate personality traits."

T. Powell (2011), Finance and Management, ICAEW, "Stop Groupthink Damaging Your Business."

A. Priestland & R. Hanig (2005), Harvard Business Review, "Developing First-Level Leaders."

D.A. Ready & J.A. Conger (2007), Harvard Business Review, "Talent management – make your company a talent factory."

D.A. Ready, L.A. Hill & J.A. Conger (2008), Harvard Business Review, "Winning the Race for Talent in Emerging Markets."

T. Rockstuhl, J.H. Dulebohn, S. Ang & L.M. Shore (2012), Journal of Applied Psychology, "Leader-member exchange (LMX) and culture: a meta-analysis of correlates of LMX across 23 countries."

P. Rosinski (2003), "Coaching across cultures: new tools for leveraging national, corporate and professional differences." Nicholas Brealey.

E.H. Schein (2010, 4th ed.), "Organisational Culture and Leadership." Jossey-Bass.

E.R. Schnell & A. L. Hammers (1997), "Introduction to the FIRO-B® instrument in organisations." OPP.

T. Schwartz & C. McCarthy (2007), Harvard Business Review, "Manage Your Energy, Not Your Time."

K.W. Thomas (1992), Journal of Organizational Behavior, "Conflict and conflict management: reflections and update."

F. Trompenaars & P. Woolliams (2003), "Business across Cultures." Capstone.

F. Trompenaars & C. Hampden-Turner (1998), "Riding the Waves of Culture: understanding diversity in global business." Nicholas Brealey.

F. Vermeulen (2011), Business Strategy Review, "Five Mistaken Beliefs Business Leaders Have about Innovation."

M. Vinson, C. Pung & J. M. Gonzalez-Blanch (2006), McKinsey Global Survey, "Organising for successful change management."

J. Whitmore (2009, 4th ed.), "Coaching for Performance: GROWing human potential and purpose. The principles and practices of coaching and leadership." Nicholas Brealey.

A. Zaleznik, (1992, reprint), Harvard Business Review, "Managers and Leaders: are they different?"